Faith Forming Faith

Faith Forming Faith

Bringing New Christians to Baptism and Beyond

PAUL E. HOFFMAN

Foreword by Diana Butler Bass

CASCADE *Books* · Eugene, Oregon

FAITH FORMING FAITH
Bringing New Christians to Baptism and Beyond

Cascade Books
An Imprint of Wipf and Stock Publishers
199 W. 8th Ave., Suite 3
Eugene, OR 97401

www. wipfandstock.com

ISBN 13: 978-1-61097-527-8

Cataloging-in-Publication data:

Hoffman, Paul E.

    Faith forming faith : bringing new Christians to baptism and beyond /
Paul E. Hoffman ; with a foreword by Diana Butler Bass.

    xx + 110 p. ; 23 cm. Including bibliographical references.

    ISBN 13: 978-1-61097-527-8

    1. Initiation rites — religious aspects. 2. Baptism. I. Bass, Diana Butler,
1959–. II. Title.

BX8335 .H75 2012

Manufactured in the U.S.A.

*To the faithful women, men, and children of God
at Phinney Ridge Lutheran Church
in Seattle, Washington:
past, present, and future.*

Contents

Contents

Foreword

SEVERAL YEARS ago, I happened to be in Seattle on the night Phinney Ridge Lutheran Church hosted a dinner for inquirers who were embarking on The WAY, the congregation's year-long process of deepening Christian life. Pastor Paul Hoffman invited me to join them as they began their pilgrimage of learning, reflection, prayer, worship, and service.

The large group who gathered to mark the start of the journey was young—many in their early twenties. Those at my table shared stories of what had brought them to the church; they told tales of searching, questions, kindness, justice, and friendship. I quizzed them, "What do you think of a church that asks you to engage in a year-long process of learning faith?" One fellow laughed, "Someone told me that Jesus taught his followers for three years! If the church asked less than a year, I'd think I was being cheated."

In a world of many choices, a world that is post-religious and increasingly post-Christian, it is important to grasp what that young man was saying: Faith is costly. It takes time to explore and engage. What is truly worthwhile is not flashy or fast. The Christian way of life is a journey. He was not a church member. He did not know much about the Bible or liturgy. But he knew that. I suspect that he is not alone in his insight.

So many churches today are desperate to fill empty pews or maintain decaying buildings that they will invest in whatever is the latest program or quick fix that promises to solve their problems. But they are missing the point, perhaps even "cheating" those who are searching for a meaningful life. What the people of Phinney

Ridge have discovered is simple, lovely, and profound. As it was in ancient times, being a follower of The WAY and inviting others to follow The WAY is the most compelling thing God's people can do. There are no shortcuts. Being an authentic, hospitable, faithful community of liturgy and life is meaningful church for the twenty-first century—and the sort of congregation that touches the longings of a searching people.

In *Faith Forming Faith*, Paul Hoffman is not trying to fix anything. Instead of fixing the church, he urges God's people to be the church as he shares the wisdom of what one congregation has learned on a journey to embody the way of Christ.

Diana Butler Bass,
author, *Christianity After Religion: The End of Church
and the Beginning of a New Spiritual Awakening*

Preface

IN 1960 at Phinney Ridge Lutheran Church in Seattle, Washington, the stirring of the Spirit's breath was evident. At that time, it was one of the largest and most prominent Lutheran churches on the West Coast. A haven for first- and second-generation Norwegians and other Scandinavians, it was well known throughout the western half of the United States. Lutheran folks moving from Minnesota or North Dakota to Seattle for work or adventure were often advised by their hometown pastors to become members of this parish before they ever packed a suitcase. In 1960, even in Seattle, it was not just fashionable to be a part of a Christian community—it was expected. The turbulent, questioning seventies were still a decade away and the skepticism of Vietnam, Watergate, and a host of other social and political upheavals had not yet taken their toll on North American congregational life.

Church attendance and participation may have been fashionable and expected, but people also attended for different reasons than they do now, fifty years later. Like many other congregations, Phinney was a part of "American Christendom," an unlikely and unintentional manifestation of what Samuel Simon Schmucker had envisioned in the early 1800s when he imagined the Lutheran Church as the common national church of the new nation. In the 1960s, people were at church primarily because they were born into it. It was what one *did* in mid-twentieth century North America. As Scandinavians whose religious experiences had been steeped in the state church model, not only were they expected to be there, they also had certain expectations of church from their northern European heritages. Baptize, marry, bury. Teach the Bible and its important moral lessons for a life of civility.

By 1990, things had changed radically among Protestants in general and at Phinney Ridge in particular. The underlying social, political, and religious forces occasioning the changing face of church are another topic for another book. But suffice it to say that among other phenomena, these three factors all contributed to Lutheranism's decline on Phinney Ridge. The children of baby boomers became a questioning generation who often found themselves on the receiving end of unsatisfactory doctrinal responses. These responses lacked nuance and the ambiguous possibilities that the late sixties, seventies, and eighties in American culture had inculcated in the children it had spawned. The pat answers did not satisfy and often drove those of the post-World War II era away. Second, there was social permission to enjoy the lure of the great outdoors in the magnificent Pacific Northwest, even on Sundays. Finally, a changing ethic that saw church as peripheral rather than central to social and civil discourse helped empty the pews. Astute lay leaders and a newly called, thoughtful, and mission-minded pastor saw by 1990 that something had to change if Phinney Ridge Lutheran Church was going to survive.

This book is the story of that change. The mystery of God's reviving breath stirring though our congregation and community and propelling us into a new ministry for a new day is too wonderful to keep to ourselves. The practice of the Adult Catechumenate as a means by which new Christians are brought to the waters of baptism is the primary lens through which the practice of our ministry is viewed. The parish's renewal has taken place despite living in a time of continuing church decline and disintegration. It could not have happened without the incredible commitment, perseverance, and faith in Christ that our forebears in this ministry held at the very center of their lives. What we have inherited in the current era of our ministry could only have happened because of the strong resolve and faithful foundation that was laid and maintained before most of us were ever on the scene. Those foundations were laid in the most challenging of times.

It is to the faithful women and men of Phinney Ridge's early years that this book is dedicated. *Faith Forming Faith* is possible only because of our congregation's strong and faithful heritage as it waded its way in ministry through the twentieth century, one of the most quickly changing times in the history of humanity. And of course, underlying every assumption of this book, *Faith Forming Faith* is possible only because of the breath of God's Holy Spirit, living and active among us. Through that Spirit's breath, we learn over and over again of the love and commitment of Jesus Christ, the Lord of the Church, whose death and resurrection makes all things new, and anything possible.

Acknowledgments

WHILE IN large part this story has been about the ministry of one particular parish, it is more truthfully the culmination of my own faith formation that has taken place across the years. It began with my baptism at Christ Lutheran Church in Shrewsbury, Pennsylvania. I owe my family and all Christ's people there a debt of gratitude for their early nurture and continuing support. Before Phinney Ridge Lutheran in Seattle, I have served three other Lutheran parishes: Grace Lutheran in Lincoln, Nebraska; Christ the Servant Lutheran in Allen, Texas; and Sinai Lutheran in Fremont, Nebraska. Each congregation contributed in its own way to preparing me for the ministry that I am now privileged to lead in Seattle. For the incredible trust that the people of Phinney Ridge have placed in my leadership, I simply stand in awe. The fulfillment of this work could never have been so joyous had it not been for the partnership in ministry that I share with the Reverend Beverly Piro, our Associate Pastor. This story is as much hers as it is mine, and I am grateful for every experience in parish life that we have had the privilege to share.

Of Bowls, Bones, and Breath

The hand of the LORD was upon me, and he brought me out by the Spirit of the LORD, and set me down in the midst of the valley; it was full of bones. And he led me round among them; and behold, there were very many upon the valley; and lo, they were very dry. And he said to me, "Son of man, can these bones live?" And I answered, "O Lord GOD, you know." Again he said to me, "Prophesy to these bones, and say to them, O dry bones, hear the word of the LORD. Thus says the Lord GOD to these bones: Behold, I will cause breath to enter you, and you shall live. And I will lay sinews upon you, and will cause flesh to come upon you, and cover you with skin, and put breath in you, and you shall live; and you shall know that I am the LORD."

So I prophesied as I was commanded; and as I prophesied, there was a noise, and behold, a rattling; and the bones came together, bone to its bone. And as I looked, there were sinews on them, and flesh had come upon them, and skin had covered them; but there was no breath in them. Then he said to me, "Prophesy to the breath, prophesy, son of man, and say to the breath, Thus says the Lord GOD: Come from the four winds, O breath, and breathe upon these slain, that they may live." So I prophesied as he commended me, and the breath came into them, and they lived, and stood upon their feet, an exceedingly great host.

Then he said to me, "Son of man, these bones are the whole house of Israel. Behold, they say, 'Our bones are dried up, and our hope is lost; we are clean cut off.' Therefore prophesy, and say to them, Thus says the

Lord GOD: Behold, I will open your graves, and raise you from your graves, O my people; and I will bring you home into the land of Israel. And you shall know that I am the LORD, when I open your graves, and raise you from your graves, O my people. And I will put my Spirit within you, and you shall live, and I will place you in your own land; then you shall know that I, the LORD, have spoken, and I have done it, says the LORD."

Ezekiel 37:1–14, RSV

THERE WAS an unfortunate incident at our church during the Lenten season. The baptismal bowl was shattered. It happened while the children's choir was rehearsing a Hebrew dance that was to punctuate the response to the reading of the Exodus story at the Vigil of Easter. The Vigil was only a few weeks away when the unthinkable happened. It was nobody's fault. Truly. The grapevine stepping line of third, fourth, fifth, and sixth graders just got a little too close to the font, a well-propelled hip went crashing into it, and, as if in slow motion, the entire thing crashed to the ground: water, handblown glass, wooden stand and all. The water was everywhere, and the glass shattered into what seemed a million pieces. They sparkled like stars on the brand new carpet, now soaked with a couple of gallons of last Sunday's water.

You can imagine the reaction of the children. They were mortified. No one moved. All eyes were on the pastor. What would he do? How would he respond? What would his words to them be about the demolition of what they had been taught over and over again was the central symbol of their faith?

Just as this was all taking place, the first and second graders were entering the sanctuary to join their older friends for the weekly closing worship together on the steps. They saw it and heard it all: the slowly tipping font, the crashing bowl and splashing waters, the children's initial shrieks of horror, and then the dead silence.

The first grader leading the line of the entering group looked up at our Children and Family Minister and said, "I don't have any bones." It was his way of saying what everyone else was feeling, "I think I'm going to faint."

Certainly without the waters of baptism, the church is faint. It has no bones. It cannot live. Ministering in one of the most unchurched cities of the United States, Phinney Ridge Lutheran congregation has discovered a way that opens the airways for the breath of God to blow through the dry, dry valley of a postmodern church in Seattle, Washington, and bring that church to life. This is the story of bones and breath, the work of God, and the work of God's people.

I

The Gospel according to Kathryn

KATHRYN WAS FILLED WITH the breath of God's Spirit and gifted with renewed bones as she rose to a new life in Christ from the womb of the baptismal font. Her new birth had given her many things, but chief among them was a strong spine. As the ancient church so wisely discerned, baptism is not a magical life-changing event that takes place in a single moment of sacramental washing. Rather, it is an ongoing, mystical process with a beginning, a middle, and a never-ending future. The catechumenate, with its intentional time of preparation for baptism, gives eternal breath and helps form strong, lasting spiritual bones. New children of God, both infants and adults, are best prepared to live out their baptismal covenant in everyday life through the preparations that the catechumenate provides. The ancient church knew this and gave us their model to follow. Its time-tested process certainly formed a sturdy theological backbone for Kathryn.

Ask anyone who was in leadership at the time and they will tell you that the congregational forum at which Kathryn gave her testimony was the transformational moment catapulting Phinney Ridge Lutheran Church in Seattle, Washington, into its new and present era of ministry. The forum was organized during Sunday morning adult education time in order to continue a conversation that had begun several months before. The agenda was to consider extending an invitation to the one hundred men and women of Tent City to spend three months encamped on our front lawn, beginning just a few weeks before Christmas.

Tent City is a well-organized, long-standing coalition of self-governing homeless people who have banded together for safety, community, and advocacy. They refer to themselves as "houseless," not "homeless." Over the years since their beginnings, the political situation had evolved in such a way that city ordinance permitted Tent City to encamp within the city limits, but only at places where they had been invited, and for no longer than ninety days in any one spot. So it fell largely to the churches of Seattle to be their advocates and hosts. No other Lutheran congregation in Seattle had ever taken the challenge, and we found ourselves moved into the conversation by the most interesting of voices, the voice of a third grader.

The previous spring, the Wednesday evening Bread for the Journey class had taken a field trip to a neighboring church that was hosting Tent City. The elementary kids and a few parents went for a tour and conversation with those houseless persons in residency at a nearby United Methodist Church. Bread for the Journey is our Wednesday evening pan-generational, choral, worship, educational, and fellowship program. Before the night of our field trip, none of us could have imagined the deepened education and fellowship that would bear fruit among us. Matthew 25:35—"I was a stranger and you welcomed me"—was about to come to life among us, revived by the Holy Spirit's breath. On the way home from our field trip to Tent City, that still, small, third-grade voice went something like this: "Pastor, when can our congregation have Tent City at *our* church?"

There were enough adults within earshot, including two key staff people. It was clear to us in this small circle that this was the voice of the Holy Spirit. We couldn't let the idea rest.

Six months later, we were in a congregational forum proposing what at first had seemed like the most remote of possibilities. As unlikely as it seemed, the idea of hosting Tent City was gaining momentum and many were beginning to believe that it could actually happen. But welcoming the stranger, as theologically and scripturally sound as it was, also seemed even for a hopeful realist unlikely at best. This was going to be ministry in real life, not in theological theory. We are an upper-middle-class congregation whose ministry includes a childcare center that daily serves seventy children. Our well-manicured, block-long property on the summit of Phinney Ridge is one of the few green spaces in the neighborhood. It was hard for even the most imaginative and liberal proponent of the Gospel to escape the hard truth that people living in adjoining million-dollar view homes would not instantly embrace our invitation to the homeless as a magnificent idea.

So in preparation for the forum and for the certain possibility of well-reasoned and well-intentioned objections *against* hosting Tent City, the staff and leadership had discussed our strategy for addressing opponents: be good listeners, remain non-anxious, offer insights, don't get into a power struggle. Most of all, point to the mandates of Scripture and stay grounded in the treasure of our Lutheran theology—God's unconditional grace for all. We had even gone so far as to rehearse responses to those who might threaten to leave our congregation, should we choose to move ahead and invite our brothers and sisters in Christ who live in Tent City to join us for the holy days of Christmas and into the new year.

But we hadn't prepared ourselves for newly baptized Kathryn.

Kathryn was one of many adults who, over the years since 1994, chose to participate in the annual cycle of preparation for baptism through Phinney Ridge Lutheran's contemporary appropriation of the ancient Christian practice of the Adult Catechumenate. As her comments were about to reveal, Kathryn was baptized by total immersion. Not only had she gone all the way under the waters at the moment of her baptism, but also the waters had totally covered her with a new way of understanding her life, her faith, and her relationship with the body of Christ.

3

After listening to the conversation at the congregational forum with restrained patience, Kathryn stood in the assembly and took a deep breath. "I can't believe the objections that I'm hearing to this opportunity. I can't believe them because, as I was preparing for my baptism last year, this is what you told me that being a baptized child of God would mean. You told me that to be a disciple of Christ meant to care for those less fortunate. To reach out to those in need. To share God's love with all people. That's what you taught me it means to be a baptized disciple of Jesus."

And then Kathryn said the most amazing thing of all, the thing that none of us had anticipated hearing—and for which no one had rehearsed a response. "So if we decide that we can't invite Tent City to be on our front lawn, I will have to leave this congregation. If Tent City can't be here, then I can't either, because what you have taught me about who we are as the people of God and what it means to be one of you will not be true."

The room fell silent. For all intents and purposes, the conversation was over. To be sure, there were still opponents to address and details to be worked out, but in that single moment of testimony, God spoke to us through Kathryn, and, as 2 Corinthians 5:17 promises, the old had passed away and the new had come. In Christ we were made a new creation. The voice of that third-grade child three months prior was now amplified by the voice of a new child of God. Before long, the voices of God's people at Phinney Ridge Lutheran Church joined together to reach out and invite another community of God's people who happened to live in tents to join us in the continuing discovery of what it means to live as people of the resurrected Christ.

Had Phinney Ridge Lutheran Church not been a congregation practicing the Adult Catechumenate, I believe that we would not have been ready to reach out and welcome Tent City. Bringing new people to faith through baptismal preparation has meant much more for us than simply growing the congregation. It has opened our eyes to a new way of being the people of God in a new age with a new paradigm. Forming others in faith has formed *us* for ministry and outreach. How those two things are irrevocably connected and intertwined is, in large part, the theme of this book. Phinney Ridge is not an extraordinary place. We see ourselves as a typical neighborhood Protestant congregation facing many of the same challenges that affect any other ministry in North America a decade into the new millennium. We do have the additional challenge that not every congregation faces of being located in a liberal, institutionally suspect setting, where less than 10 percent of the population claims any formal affiliation with a faith community. Fifteen years ago, when we began the practice of forming new Christians for baptismal living, not many congregations believed that their communities of faith were congregations that could benefit from such a ministry. But the creeping tide of secularism, the growing mistrust of institutionalized faith, and the general decline of church across the country all collide to make a process of faith formation a valuable option to consider. Our catechumenal story is the story of how, through the baptismal preparation of new Christians, *we as a congregation* are formed in faith and strengthened for mission in the world, over and over again.

2

What Is The WAY?

SINCE THE MID-1990S, MEN and women just like Kathryn have visited our congregation and expressed an interest in learning more about following Jesus. Subsequently, they have been invited to participate in the yearlong process of faith formation that we call The WAY. There is nothing all that mysterious about what we do in The WAY. Our pattern of forming people in faith borrows from and builds upon the disciplines of the ancient church that have been under development since the third century. In a word, The WAY offers people an apprenticeship into faith in Christ. It is designed both for those who have never been baptized as well as those have at one time or another practiced a life of faith but have walked off, stomped off, or been chased off. In our annual cycle of baptismal preparation we even include persons with an active life of faith who are transferring to us from other Lutheran congregations. Wherever they are in their continuing walk of faith with Christ, The WAY offers them the opportunity to experience a fruitful period of spiritual enrichment.

Kathryn came at the recommendation of a supervisor in her law office. Having just lost a husband in a tragic automobile accident, Kathryn was longing for a spiritual center through which to find meaning and purpose for her life as a young widow. She had only tangential Christian Science experiences in her childhood, but other than that, no exposure to the Christian faith. Her supervisor knew about The WAY at our church and suggested that she visit. Perhaps what it had to offer her would be helpful in her healing, he suggested.

Other people come for other reasons, of course. Many come simply as newcomers to Seattle, hoping to find a Lutheran church like their old one in Omaha or Houston—strong preaching, good youth programs, and not too much talk about money. Others come because a friend invites them. Some simply wander in.

As people begin to express an interest in life in Christ with our congregation, we encourage them to consider participation in the coming cycle of The WAY. Sunday evening gatherings begin in the fall, so all throughout the late spring and summer months the staff and members of the parish are busy pointing newcomers, inquirers, visitors, and the unbaptized to this process.

The formal organization of the catechumenate and the materials that our denomination offers in a series called *Welcome to Christ* suggest that there are four distinct stages of catechumenal ministry:

- Inquiry
- Catechumenate
- Baptismal Preparation
- Baptismal Living, sometimes called Mystagogy

We have been known to say over and over again that the process of the catechumenate is "rich and messy." It is rich because of its immersion in Scripture and life in Christ. It is messy because it involves real people with real needs and real schedules whose lives and experiences in faith seldom follow the neat, linear pattern that the stages above suggest.

Laying out these stages of the catechumenate as a fixed paradigm risks oversimplification. While they are helpful to bear in mind, it must also be considered that real life is bound to be messy. Real people—with real lives, personalities, and questions—make their way through these stages as they consider coming to faith. To suggest that everyone follow the same path at the same pace is naïve. The stages make a great leadership framework, but in our experience they are foundations to which we rarely refer with the candidates.

An example from our workshop teaching will illustrate the point. When training congregational leaders or seminarians about the theological underpinnings of the catechumenate and its four stages, I will frequently give each person a blank piece of square white paper. Here are the instructions: fold your paper into four distinctive parts, none of which can be equal. Be creative! Now, hand your paper to the person sitting next to you. The next step in the illustration is to have the group take notes about the four stages on their newly acquired notepaper. By telling them that they are using someone else's construction to record information about stages that are neither linear nor neatly divided into equal parts strongly makes the point. Catechumenal stages are defined by those inquiring, not by those in leadership. They vary widely. They can be long or short, creative or mundane; but they will be unique, as all God's people are unique. Rich, but messy. One can only speak about the stages in the most general terms.

So, roughly speaking, our fall Sunday evening small group sessions represent the stage of Inquiry. People who express an interest in membership, in learning more about baptism for themselves or their children, or who desire a closer relationship with the body of Christ through our congregation are invited to gather six to eight times in October, November, and early December.

Depending on where these people are in their own lives of faith, they connect at different places along The WAY. For some, it is clearly review time. The education or formation that takes place has more to do with how we live our lives together in Christ in this particular community. For persons new to faith, it is certainly a time of inquiry. We are very clear that attending The WAY at this stage implies no obligation to join our parish, to be baptized, to become a part of the larger Christian church. This is a time of honest inquiry, to see who Christians are and how we try to live our lives. We work very hard at keeping both the front and the back doors open for people to come and go freely.

The Sunday evening format is straightforward and relaxed. The inquirers gather for a hearty, family style meal that includes the lay group leaders, potential sponsors for this cycle, at least one of the pastors, and a few men or women who would otherwise eat alone and enjoy the opportunity to share a meal in community. Children are encouraged to be a part of the mealtime. Table prayer, a new discipline for those new to faith, is modeled by seasoned Christians at the table, as is the art of table hospitality and conversation. Our goal with the meal is to help people feel welcome, offer them a place to belong, and create a space in which relationships with other Christians can begin to form and take shape. One of the reasons that we have been so encouraging to folks who are transferring into our congregation to also be participants in The WAY is that their presence adds an additional layer of Christian tradition and experience. "At our former church, we . . ." is a piece of conversation that brings breadth and depth to what we as a single congregation have to offer.

After dinner, childcare is provided by the paid parish childcare worker or a familiar volunteer. When children and parents recognize a welcome face from their Sunday morning time at church, their anxiety eases. The level of trust with new, young parents that their child is being well cared for is a key ingredient to freeing their hearts and minds to concentrate on the work that is about to begin.

For the next hour, led by a lay Bible study leader, small groups of six to eight persons meet in separate rooms. The pastors do not participate, nor do they visit these groups. The topic at hand is the Gospel text from the morning's liturgy and the sermon. Catechists are either provided with or formulate a few leading questions to get the group started, but the idea is to address the questions and concerns that the group members bring. There are no planned outcomes, other than that the group have an open, honest, confidential conversation about their shared lives in Christ, springing from the morning's texts.

Over the years, the questions have been amazing. They run a wide gamut.

"What is a prayer? Why would I pray one? To whom would it be addressed? How would I get started?"

"Do I have to believe that Jesus is the divine Son of God in order to keep worshiping here?"

"What do you really mean when you say, 'Eat his body, drink his blood'?"

"Will I ever find the answers to why both my parents beat me when I was a child if God is a God of love?"

"Is there anything here that can help me be a better father? Husband?"

Without a pastor in the room, the groups do considerable work in sharing with one another the struggles, joys, and responses they have experienced through life in Christ. This is faith formation, not faith *information*. There is never any work in the small group that looks or sounds like this: "The meaning of this passage is . . ."

In their small groups, men and women who have lived the faith share what they have learned and known to be God's truth revealed to them in the Scriptures. They also attempt to apply the Scriptures to a complex, troubling world as they have come to understand them in this community of faith.

At the conclusion of the small groups, all who have attended gather for a five-minute recap that includes announcements and a closing prayer. Little by little, as the fall progresses and as the Christmas holidays give way to a new year, we all enjoy watching that closing circle of prayer grow. Since there is no set curriculum, we allow and encourage the flexibility of new men and women joining our small group process throughout the fall and early winter. It is not until the Lenten season begins, six weeks before Easter, that the group for this year's cycle is closed, and newcomers and seekers who visit the congregation thereafter are pointed to next fall's cycle as their starting point.

As is the case with most liturgical denominations, the Evangelical Lutheran Church in America has corresponding rites that punctuate the candidate's walk toward baptism or its affirmation at the Easter Vigil. Whether Lutheran, United Methodist, or Mennonite, these rites are easily adapted to a wide range of parish settings and worship practices. It is possible to practice the catechumenate in congregations of all sizes and in faith communities with a wide variety of worship styles.

More than anything else, these rites, however they are practiced, delineate the four stages and assist the candidates in assessing their own developing state of heart and mind. The rites help them discern whether they feel genuinely called to a lifetime of discipleship. We do not apologize for the simple truth that this level of serious, life-transforming discernment takes time.

Prior to the beginning of Lent, candidates who indicate their intent to continue are assigned sponsors who will walk with them throughout the Sunday evening gatherings and all other aspects of The WAY. In consultation with the candidates, the sponsors are chosen, recruited, and matched by the pastors. A later chapter will deal with recruitment, training, and nurture offered to sponsors, but for now suffice it to say that as the years of The WAY have progressed, it has become easier to recruit sponsors. We find that parishioners are particularly eager to walk side by side with another adult who is new to the Christian faith and preparing for baptism.

The first of the public rites, held at the regular Sunday worship of the congregation, is the Rite of Welcome. At this rite, the candidates receive a ritual welcome to the process of The WAY by the entire congregation. They are given a Bible for their further study of the Scriptures as their journey of faith intensifies. And, most significant of all, in this rite they receive at the hand of their sponsors the sign of the cross.

Receive the cross on your shoulders,
  that you may bear the gentle yoke of Christ.
Receive the cross on your eyes,
  that you may see the light of Christ, illumination for
  the world.
Receive the cross on your feet,
  that you may walk in the way of Christ.[1]

With this public, ritual action and blessing, the candidates are reminded that the way of following Jesus is the way of the cross. They learn in a concrete, physical way that as a disciple of Christ, their lives, like the lives of millions of Christians before them, are marked with the sign of the cross. As early as the third century, Tertullian attests that men and women received the sacred sign of the cross on their bodies in connection with baptism and its preparation.[2] Rites such as those used by catechumenal congregations are rites with deep roots in the Church's history and practice. They may be updated and reappropriated, but they are neither new nor without historic precedent.

There is something mysteriously powerful about the rituals that accompany The WAY, just as there is with all scripturally grounded liturgical action. In the first place, these rituals are unique to the Church and its mission in the world. There is no place else in life where one could imagine receiving the blessing of a sponsor's presence, touch, and prayerful support as one receives it through these rituals and words of public worship. Such rituals as the Rite of Welcome also convey to the candidates the intensity of their response to follow the call of Jesus, simply by the fact that the rite is public. The presence of the body of Christ as they make the progressive steps toward baptism or its affirmation reminds them—often in ways they do not yet fully understand—that their relationship with Christ and Christ's church may be personal, but it is not private. God's people receive and offer the gifts of grace *in community.*

1. Nelson et al., eds., *Welcome to Christ*, 11.
2. Turner, *Hallelujah Highway*, 30.

It is through such public affirmations and rites that The WAY belongs to all the people of God, not just the candidates, sponsors, and catechists. Men and women who worship will tell powerful stories about what it means to them to see others beginning to embrace the faith that they have practiced—and perhaps have taken for granted—since their birth. For each worshiper, the presence of inquirers among us gives the joy and the confidence of having responded to the Great Commission Christ gives in Matthew 28. It is also joyful testimony to God's answer to prayer, since seeing these men and women for whom we have prayed standing before us is indisputable evidence of God's work in the world through us.

The Sunday evening gatherings during Lent, now weekly, are much the same as those held earlier in the fall and winter. The difference during this time of intense preparation is in the depth of each person's walk as it has developed over the months. More time is allowed for reflection between the paired candidates and sponsors. In the small groups, the questions have also intensified and deepened and commitments to shared prayer for one another throughout the week increase the bonds of intimacy and community among the participants.

In Sunday worship, Lent provides a rich scriptural palette of stories of those seeking faith. Abraham and Sarah, Moses, Isaiah, the man born blind, Nicodemus, and the disciples themselves are coming to terms with what it means to follow God.

In Sunday evening discussion groups, questions such as, "What are you seeking from Christ and Christ's Church?" are generated by the morning's text of Nicodemus coming to Jesus by night (John 3). "Out of what darkness and into what light is God calling you?" corresponds with the morning reading of the man born blind from John 9. As Lazarus is called forth from the tomb, beginning questions for discussion the Sunday evening of Lent 5 might be: "At the coming Vigil of Easter, what will die within you?" or "What new life do you anticipate on the other side of the font, having heard this story of Lazarus and Jesus?"

Various weekly Lenten rites offer the candidates further opportunities to receive the congregation's prayers and blessings as their baptisms or affirmations draw near. These rites also act as checkpoints for the candidates to continue to discern and affirm that seeking a lifelong commitment to Christ is indeed their intention. Gifts that symbolize the essence of our faith are given during these rites: a copy of the catechism, a copy of the Apostles' Creed, and a book of worship.

As the words and actions of catechumenal rites are enacted among the congregation and candidates, as gifts are given and received, and as the small group work of study and prayer continues and intensifies, men and women preparing for the Easter Vigil come to realize that the journey of life with Christ is just that—a journey. The witness of catechists, sponsors, and other congregational members sharing their own struggles and doubts enables men and women preparing for baptism to more fully understand that preparation does not mean having the right answers to faith's large questions, nor reaching a point of doctrinal clarity. The WAY's gift is first and foremost the assurance that baptism is incorporation into a community of Christ. This community *continues* to struggle, doubt, question, and discern how the ancient words of Scripture and the Spirit of the resurrected Jesus among us equip us for witness in the world.

In our understanding of baptism and in our teaching and interpreting it to those new to faith, we emphasize again and again that grace means God's acceptance of us, not our acceptance of God. It is an acceptance that has the dimension of a once-and-forever act in the sacrament of baptism on a specific date, time, and place. But it is also the gracious gift of continuing acceptance, and God's holy presence in a life of struggle, suffering, and pain *every single day* of our lives. Each step of the way we emphasize the gem of the Protestant Reformation's rediscovery of grace. It is God who unconditionally welcomes and receives us. The decision to be baptized or to live in continuing affirmation of baptism is a "yes" to a God who in Christ has already said—and continually says—"yes" to us: "Welcome. I love you. You belong to me."

Even with all this time of participation and preparation, the candidates, especially those who have never experienced the Vigil of Easter, cannot yet have a clear idea of exactly what lies ahead for them. They have developed an incredible sense of trust, and care must be taken at every step of the way to earn and maintain that trust. Questions that inquirers bring must be treated with the utmost respect, and there is much more to be gained by an honest response—"We don't know," or "We *can't* know"—than a pat, doctrinal response that avoids the difficulties and ambiguities that life beneath the cross engenders.

In a trusting setting such as this, Kathryn learned what baptism would mean *for her*. She was, of course, given the opportunity to learn what it means from a Lutheran perspective and how it is grounded in and translated from the Scriptures into contemporary life. But the opportunity to question and reflect, to be supported by others in her small group and by the congregation through the rites of The WAY's annual process built strong baptismal bones for her. They were the kinds of bones that allowed her just six months later to stand in the assembly of the congregation at a moment of discernment and speak the truth and the power of the Holy Spirit's guidance.

In a later chapter, we will turn our attention to the events of the Easter Vigil and make the baptismal journey with men and women of The WAY whose lives are about to pass through the Red Sea of Phinney Ridge Lutheran Church's baptismal font. In that font, as with every font everywhere, they will make the passage from death to life, a new life in Christ.

3

Reaching Out by Reaching In

REACHING OUT OFTEN BEGINS by reaching in. This was the case in our story as it unfolded in the 1990s. Before we were able to offer a ministry leading to baptism to adults like Kathryn, our congregation needed to be convinced that there was a need to evangelize. It also needed to be convinced that the catechumenate was a reasonable approach by which to do so. We wanted to be able to offer adult seekers like Kathryn, who had never before known life in Christ, the grace and comfort of the Holy Spirit to bring healing and hope to her. But we also wanted to help her better understand that life in Christ not only brings hope for her but also *through* her. Becoming Christian includes embracing service to the world in Jesus' name. That loving service will in turn bring the hope of the Gospel to others.

Our congregation first needed to see that not everyone knew these fundamentals of faith as they did. Not everyone had been born into a Christian home. If the church was to continue to grow and thrive, there was a need to retool for ministry to a new, unchurched generation.

The evidence that there was such a need was overwhelming, if one was willing to see it. By 1990, a congregation's sanctuary that could barely accommodate the number of people attending three Sunday morning services in 1965 was now, just twenty-five years later, averaging less than three hundred worshipers each

16

Sunday, spread across two services. The parish's pastor at the time, Pastor Don Maier, had been a missionary in Ghana and had a zealous heart for the spread of the Gospel. He, too, recognized the need for renewal and a time of rebuilding, but was not entirely sure *how* such renewal might occur.

On reflecting on this particular time in the congregation's history, Don observes, "In the early 1990s, we were a congregation strong in faith and resources, despite the loss of membership since 1965. What we needed was the confidence that we had something important into which people who visited could be invited, and a structure to support their growth in faith once they were with us." Don recalls a "Friendship Sunday" early in his tenure as the new pastor at Phinney. "It was a huge success. People brought their friends, and not just folks they knew who skipped a week at their own Methodist or Presbyterian churches. They brought people who were unchurched. Seekers. The church was full."

But the following Sunday, it was back to business as usual. There was no structure in place to support inquirers, not the people from "Friendship Sunday" nor those who visited the congregation for an ordinary Sunday morning service. They were with us, then they were gone.

Like so many pastors in the early nineties, Pastor Maier found himself awash in the tides of two powerful movements surging through the waters of Lutheranism. One was the Church Growth Movement, the other the Liturgical Renewal Movement. Having been a missionary in his first call, Don approached ministry from a mission standpoint in each call that he served after returning to the States. "We have a Gospel to share and a Great Commission from our Lord Jesus," Don reflects, "but most Lutheran churches grew only if and when someone visited and expressed their desires to become a part of the congregation. In most Lutheran churches, including Phinney, there was no structure in place through which to welcome new people." Nor was there a mechanism to tend to their spiritual growth and development. In a city such as Seattle, where churches had been shrinking for thirty years or so, even those who wandered into church seeking "something spiritual" were often without the basic foundational elements of Christian life. They didn't know its Bible stories, its music, its theologies, or its movement from worship to mission in the world. What they did know was that they felt called and comfortable to be among other Christians.

In his Sermon on the Mount, Jesus speaks of those who have little or no foundation underlying their lives of faith:

> Everyone then who hears these words of mine and acts on them will be like a wise man who built his house on rock. The rain fell, the floods came, and the winds blew and beat on that house, but it did not fall, because it had been founded on rock. And everyone who hears these words of mine and does not act on them will be like a foolish man who built his house on sand. The rain fell, the floods came, and the winds blew and beat against that house, and it fell—and great was its fall! (Matt 7:24–27)

As a practitioner of the catechumenate, I would contend that these words apply primarily to those *within* the church who need to witness to the world that God's people stand on a strong foundation. We often apply Christ's admonition only to the newcomers and seekers among the Sunday assembly. But I see them as a word of caution to those of us *already within* the fellowship of faith. Reading them as an admonition for the insiders leads to a different conclusion. The admonition compels the action of mission and outreach. Christ clearly calls those already within the household of faith to build a strong and sturdy foundation for those new to faith. Like the first grade line leader looking at the shattered baptismal bowl, like the people of Israel held in exile hearing the vision of Ezekiel, there is a need for breath to come into the bones. But without a sturdy foundation, breath can bring windy, destructive chaos rather than strong spiritual support to a new life in the community of Christ.

Our own history showed us that often after a few weeks of pastor's class or some other sort of orientation into congregational life, men and women new to parishes like Phinney Ridge soon lost interest and enthusiasm through no fault of their own. A pastor's class may give great information. It may be expedient. It may bond them to the pastor and introduce them to parish life. But it does little to introduce them to Christians who have daily vocations other than ordained ministry. Foundation building is taking place, but more is possible. The pastor's class omits the opportunity for seekers to hear other men and women who struggle share their real life conflicts and challenges of faith. The basic foundational tools of faith to begin to cultivate a new and vibrant life in Christ are best given by fellow worshipers, rather than by the theologically trained, ordained worship leader.

Pastor Maier sensed this need for person-to-person witness and testimony. His interest in growing the church, encouraged by the Church Growth Movement, had the added advantage of his interest in and passion for the liturgical renewal that was taking place in the newly formed Evangelical Lutheran Church in America. His early work at Phinney as he began ministry there in 1989 was around preaching and teaching about the sacraments and reestablishing eucharist and baptism to their central place in the weekly life of the parish.

When introduced to the catechumenate at an ecumenical conference, Pastor Maier perceived the critical junction between these two passions—the evangelical zeal for the spread of the Gospel *coupled to* a kindling fervor for the central place of sacramental life. The catechumenate was about growing the church in two dimensions—both in depth and breadth. Not only could one find in its ancient wisdom the tools for bringing more people to Christ, but one could also use its gifts and methods as a way of renewing the lives of people both old and new to the congregation. With a convicted spirit and some real pastoral courage, Pastor Maier returned from the catechumenal conference and convinced the congregation that this was God's call for the renewal of the congregation. The process began slowly and there were many opportunities for adjustments and alterations of the process across the years. In reviewing our fifteen or so years of catechumenal cycles, it can easily be seen that no two years have been exactly alike. The process of an annual cycle of faith formation at Phinney Ridge Lutheran is clearly a work in progress.

Rather than offering any more description and information just now, I would like to present some real-life stories of men and women who have been formed in faith among our congregation through this process. As we say over and over again, The WAY is about formation, not *information*, and what better way to see the formation of new or renewed Christians than to hear their stories? Through them, you can see for yourself how our contemporary adaptation of the age-old ministry of the catechumenate allowed the Spirit's breath to bring new life to all involved in the process of forming faith.

4

Transformed Lives

THE MARTIN FAMILY

ROBERT, MARIA, AND JARED came to worship for the very first time on the Sunday after Easter. They knew no one in our congregation and no one knew them. How they found us among all the churches in Seattle is still a mystery.

In the handshake line that day, Robert announced with great flourish just how glad they were to meet me since in two weeks their entire family was gathering in Seattle from across the country, and this was the place and I was the pastor whom they had chosen for infant Jared's baptism. I had never met them until this very moment.

It wasn't until later that afternoon when I made a pastoral visit in their home that the baptismal bowl shattered, at least temporarily, out from under the eager lives of these two new parents. Having been raised in the church themselves, he a Roman Catholic and she a Lutheran, they knew at some level that having their daughter baptized was the right thing to do. But having been away from the church and its ministry for over twenty years, they had remembered the ends but not necessarily the means. The idea that baptismal preparation would be an important part of the sacrament for their family was a new and unfamiliar one to them.

Their timing was unfortunate, at least in terms of our annual cycle's schedule of events. Just a week and a day prior, at the Vigil of Easter, our parish's baptismal season had culminated with baptisms of adults and children, all of whom had been in preparation across the past year.

Even though the pastoral counsel and invitation that I gave them was not what they envisioned, after a week or so of thought, Robert and Maria elected to become participants in The WAY the following fall, postponing Jared's baptism by almost twelve months, until next Easter. It made sense to them to spend some time intentionally preparing for an event that they were coming to realize was more than just a ceremony on a randomly chosen day. The idea that The WAY would give them an opportunity to consider their own relationship to Christ as adult Christians appealed to them. They loved Jared so much that they wanted what was best for him. This seemed to be it. Not simply a "drive-through" baptism, but a new way of life. The day that they signed on for The WAY, none of us could have imagined just how life-changing their journey with Jesus toward the waters of baptism would be for all of us.

Not long after The WAY began that fall, Robert came to see me. "We've never really talked much about my work, pastor," he began. "But through the Bible studies in The WAY and conversations with my sponsor, I'm beginning to see that I can't be a good baptismal daddy for my son and still keep working where I currently work."

"What is it that you do, Robert?" I asked.

"I am the manger of a club downtown. It's a strip club, actually. I think I need to look for something different. I can see that Christ loves and values all people, that my current work is exploiting women, and I want something better for my son, for my wife, and for myself."

"I agree. Do you have anything in mind?"

"Maria thinks I would make a great physical therapist. What do you think about that idea, Pastor Hoffman?"

And so began a journey that was much, much more ambitious than the original journey to a baptismal day in the life of one little boy. Robert's transformation affected him, his wife, and Jared as well. But more than that, he became a living witness to all of us who knew him and came to know his story. Not long after Jared was baptized and Robert and Maria stood before the congregation to affirm their own baptisms, they sold their home, packed up their belongings, and moved to Chicago where Robert pursued a degree in physical therapy. Through their baptismal preparation, he changed his vocation, choosing one in which he honored the body rather than objectified it.

All of this happened about ten years ago, and last summer when my wife and I passed through Robert and Maria's new hometown in upstate New York, we saw firsthand how much he loved his work, how stable and grounded their family was, and how honored he was in his community as a man of integrity. The breath of God blew over their lives, they were immersed in Christ, and, as new creations, the old had passed away, behold, the new had come.

Had the congregation answered their eagerness with something less than our intense and intentional process of Christian formation, it is likely that none of this would have happened. Instead, we all became partners of Christ in walking as people of The WAY, and God transformed life for all of us: pastor, congregation, community, couple, and child.

DIANA

Diana found herself without options. In her fifty or so years of life, she had searched everywhere for some sort of meaning and purpose. Meditation, Jungian psychology, substance abuse, intellectual pursuits, immersion in radical politics and community service all spoke to her for a while, but didn't seem to have any staying power. Alcoholics Anonymous had been as close to the church and its ministry as anything she had encountered, but until now the higher power was certainly not the God revealed in Jesus Christ.

Most of her friendship circles and searches for truth had been anti-Christian and certainly anti-institutional, so walking through the doors of our very established, very foreboding, very intentional copy of Martin Luther's "mighty fortress" took either courage or desperation. In truth, it was probably a little of both.

Diana was a worshiper who came late and left early. She wanted to find out what Christianity at this particular place and time was all about, but she certainly didn't want to risk being recognized, entangled, or more deeply invited. What she was hoping for was relief on her own terms.

A previous life of addiction, secular pursuits, and railing against "those Christian hypocrites" made it unlikely in her mind that she could actually make a connection inside a Lutheran Church. Though reluctant, she was determined. She hoped for a snippet of truth to be imparted that she could take with her back into the sphere of her secular life. Discipleship was out of the question. She simply wanted relief.

Because Diana hates to cook, the invitation to a Sunday evening meal at The WAY had a certain appeal to her. She stuck with the process for about six weeks or so the first time, then talked herself out of it, reasoning that the people at church were every bit as hypocritical and unenlightened as she had imagined. Her suspicions were confirmed: this was not what she was looking for.

A few months passed, and I phoned her to let her know how much we missed her. "This is not a guilt trip, Diana," I said. "This is a genuine invitation for you to return. We're just not the same without you."

Diana returned. The wonder and beauty of our weekly worship—its fine music and solid, Gospel-centered, relevant preaching—along with stimulating conversation in a women's book group captured her attention and led her back into a second attempt at The WAY. This time, it was an inexperienced pastoral intern's response to her question about honoring her parents that sent her back out the door. "How am I supposed to honor parents who were abusive in every way imaginable? And why should I?" The response was without nuance, and lacked the fullness of the Gospel. The pastor-in-training quickly replied, "You need to do it. It's one of the Ten Commandments." And Diana, reluctant to buy into life as a disciple of Christ in the first place, was gone again.

It was her third attempt to complete The WAY that brought her all the way to the waters of baptism at the Vigil of Easter. As the time to be baptized or affirm her baptism drew near, I asked her if she'd ever been baptized before. She found this a frankly ridiculous question. What difference did it make if she had been or not? Couldn't she just get baptized again after all the trouble she had been through, after all? I explained that we believe that baptism is a once-and-forever event and that to repeat it would be to diminish its power. She should try to find out and might start by asking her parents. "They won't remember," she responded.

Honestly, if she had not become so emotionally, intellectually, and spiritually attached to the body of Christ by this point, I think this last conversation would have sent her out the door for good. But the grace of God is powerful and effective, and through a series of conversations, she discovered that she had, after all, been baptized as an infant. "I've been a child of God all along, and never knew it," she said. When she sings, *'Twas grace that brought me safe thus far / and grace will lead me home,* it has a particular meaning and depth for her.

Though reluctant to bump up against us Christians, Diana worships almost every Sunday, right in the front pew. She has served in a variety of leadership positions and just this past spring represented our congregation at the denomination's synod assembly. Perhaps most telling of all, her business card as a professional therapist has what looks like a small gear in the upper righthand corner. It's not really a gear at all, but an acronym: C.O.G., which stands for child of God. It's her way of giving witness to her faith in a quiet and effective way that is reassuring and sustaining for her, even if those among whom she serves and works are not yet fully on board with her new life in Christ.

KEVIN AND ANZARA

Not everyone's story is as dramatic as Robert and Maria's, nor as Diana's. Kevin and Anzara were a young couple who came to us at the invitation of a coworker after the birth of their first daughter.

As a lifelong Lutheran, Anzara wondered out loud at work one day where Luisa would be baptized and how that was all going to fit together with her husband, Kevin, who grew up in a family that had never gone to church. Kevin, in fact, had never been baptized himself.

The coworker suggested our congregation as a welcome place, and the Millers came the following week. After visiting our congregation for a few months, they checked "the box," indicating that they'd like a visit from the pastor. Sitting in their home one evening after the dishes were in the dishwasher and Luisa had been put to bed for the night, I described to Kevin how people in our congregation receive an invitation to learn more about faith in Christ through The WAY, and he listened with interest. "As you prepare to have Luisa baptized and learn what that means for you as a couple, you may also come to find that this is something that you desire for yourself," I ventured. Anzara was surprised to learn that there might be a way for her faith to be reinvigorated (she had been away from the church during her college and early career years). Not only that, she and Kevin would learn more about raising a daughter in the faith together. Through Bible study, prayer, and the collegial support of a faith mentor, Kevin could be apprenticed into the faith that Anzara cherished. Work that she imagined doing herself would be supported in a way she never imagined by the process of welcome and formation in faith that we offer.

Kevin was quietly surprised to find that his questions about the faith were taken seriously. The WAY gatherings on Sunday evenings gave him an opportunity to meet other people like himself who had never really experienced Scripture, prayer, hospitality, and life in Christian community. Anzara, who had expected to go to a four- or six-week pastor's class on her own, was also beginning to see the value of a reexamination of her faith as an adult, a wife, and a mother. She was eased by what was being offered to Kevin and how he was able to receive it.

Don't get the impression that our contemporary adaptation of the catechumenate is only about Sunday evening small group ministry or Bible study. It involves the whole congregation. As we've seen earlier, on several occasions the candidates and their sponsors are brought before the congregation to receive the gifts of prayer and central symbols of our faith—the Scriptures, the Creed, a hymn. Recall that one of the first rites is the Rite of Welcome, which signifies the candidates' serious intentions to follow in the way of Christ and the congregation's pledge of support for the journey. Again, in this rite, the candidates physically receive the sign of the cross on various parts of their bodies as a tangible and liturgical reminder that the way of Jesus is the way of the cross. While the presider speaks and the congregation responds, the sponsors of each candidate offer the sign of the cross to the eyes, ears, hands, heart, and feet of those being welcomed:

> *Receive the sign of the cross on your heart, that God may dwell there by faith.*

And as their sponsors kneel before them:

> *Receive the cross on your feet, that you may walk in the way of Christ.*[1]

On the first Sunday of Lent, those preparing for baptism at the coming Vigil of Easter are invited to come before the congregation and enter their names into the Book of the Elect, thereby making public their commitment to receive the gift of baptism and the faith of this community. Standing by Kevin to share his commitment and offer support were his wife and his congregational sponsor.

Both Kevin and Anzara have later reflected on their entrance into the darkened church for the Easter Vigil. When they saw all those people gathered in the candlelight to hear the sto-

---

1. Nelson et al., eds., *Welcome to Christ*, 11.

ries of faith and then join in the celebration of Kevin and Luisa's baptisms and Anzara's affirmation, it finally occurred to them that this was a "really big deal."

Yes, it is a big deal—the biggest. The sacrament of baptism is when we believe, proclaim, and profess that God has, through the power of water and the Word, transformed all that is past, put the old life of sin to death, and raised us up to a new life in Christ. "For if we have been united with him in a death like his, we shall certainly be united with him in a resurrection like his" (Rom 6:5). The breath of God blows over the waters, over frail, dying, human bones, and gives life.

HARRISON

Dying bones leads us to the story of Harrison. A lapsed Roman Catholic who hadn't been to church in years, Harrison came at the advice of his oncologist. Having been diagnosed with pancreatic cancer, his doctor's advice was that he "get his affairs in order." Among other things, this meant for Harrison a reexamination of a long-abandoned faith and finding a place to claim his baptismal inheritance and make preparations for both his death and the promise of life to come.

Recruiting an appropriate sponsor for Harrison was a challenge of pastoral care. His sponsor would need to be solid in his own faith, loving and caring in listening and providing support, and emotionally well balanced to know that the human bonds that were about to be forged in this relationship would soon be torn apart by what St. Paul calls the last enemy, death.

Walter was the perfect choice. A man who had himself come into our congregation recently and had participated in The WAY, he was chosen because he possessed all of these qualities—and because of his own desire to have the experience of walking side by side with a person who was being awakened to life in Christ while life on earth was coming to an end.

It certainly is the case that all of our bones are dying bones. Harrison's participation in The WAY group that year brought an intensified poignancy and urgency, especially among those who were preparing for baptism. Sitting side by side with him in Sunday evening Bible studies, the members of his small group found that the words typically used to describe baptism had an added edge and clarity. Again, from St. Paul's teaching in Romans 6: "If we have died with Christ we believe that we will also live with Christ." And again: "So you also must consider yourselves dead to sin and alive to God in Jesus Christ."

By the time that Harrison affirmed his baptism, nine months after first coming to our church and asking for our help in preparing him for all that lay ahead of him, he was surrounded by a community of faith that knew him, loved him, and supported him in ways that he never imagined. Five months after his affirmation, exactly one year after he first stepped into our assembly for worship, the community gathered for his funeral and commended not a stranger, but a brother in Christ, into the care of Almighty God.

Every one of us who knew him, who walked in The WAY of Christ with him, and who suffered with him found renewal, hope, and strength for our weary, dying bones that we would not have had otherwise. Our journey of faith together over an intentional period of time, along with our shared prayers, insights, fellowship, and service, strengthened our Christian community, young and old alike. What happens in The WAY permeates all that we do in our ministry together. It is not only the candidates who are formed in faith, but all of us, over and over again.

5

What Does This Mean?

A T THE TIME OF the Reformation in Germany in the six-
teenth century, part of Luther's great disappointment with
the Church and with its pedagogy was how little people actually *understood* about their faith. He was distraught about how
little they knew of the Bible, of the basic theology that formed
the foundation beneath a life of discipleship, and how faith and
life were connected. In an effort to address the most basic understandings of the faith, Luther wrote a straightforward volume of
explanations about five basic elements of Christian understanding: the Ten Commandments, the Apostles' Creed, the Lord's
Prayer, and the two sacraments that he retained from Roman
Catholic tradition, baptism and Eucharist. Written in a question-
and-answer format, Luther's *Small Catechism* was catechetical—oral and relational—and he imagined it being used around
the family dinner table or at some other devotional time in the
home. The most frequently used device in his teaching strategy
was the question posed by the instructor: what does this mean?
Ever since, Lutherans have understood this question to be their
birthright. When we are at our best, we ask this question—about
God, about faith, about Scripture, about ourselves.

Sooner or later in our experiences of teaching others about
the wonders of the catechetical method, the question arises: what
does this mean? In other words, how do you *do* the adult cat-

echuenate in a world of overcrowded schedules and overstimu-
lated, media-driven imaginations, and among persons whose
biblical and theological understandings lack the basics? How do
you teach the Bible among biblical illiterates? Biblical skeptics?
Postmoderns? *What does this mean*—that you organize your parish and all its activities around this ancient model of evangeliza-
tion and Christian instruction?

Among the hardest concepts to grasp for those new to the
adventure of catechumenal ministry is that it is oral, relational,
and without an off-the-shelf curriculum. Just as we believe that
all liturgy is local, so we believe that the practice of the catechumenate is local. It is parish-based, person-to-person, and highly
driven by laypersons, not pastors.

The Greek root for catechumenate, *catecheo* (κατηχεω),
means "resounding in the ear." To be a catechumen is to be a
student—of Scripture, faith, and life—who *hears*. The hearing
begins, of course, in the liturgy itself, week after week. Through a
prescribed lectionary of Scripture readings, God breaks open the
Word to feed and nourish God's people for the week to come. For
those not familiar with a lectionary cycle and lectionary preaching, traditions such as our own rotate through a three-year cycle
of four Bible readings. Generally, they follow the pattern of one
reading from the Old Testament, followed by a psalm; one from
the New Testament, usually from the Epistles; and a Gospel reading. Whether one's tradition and practice is lectionary-based or
not, it is hard to imagine a service of worship without the reading
of Scripture, so the first element of the catechumenate is already
in place. The Word of God is *heard*. St. Paul could not be clearer
about this than in his Letter to the Romans:

> "*Everyone who calls on the name of the Lord shall be
> saved.*" But how are they to call on one in whom they have
> not believed? And how are they to believe in one of whom
> they have not heard? And how are they to hear without
> someone to proclaim him? . . . Faith comes through what
> is heard, and what is heard comes through the Word of
> Christ. (Rom 10:13–14, 17; emphasis mine)

Such an understanding of the importance of God's Word in the creation and formation of faith is hearty encouragement for maintaining the presence of Scripture and its proclamation at the very center of all we say and do liturgically.

Liturgy, like the catechism, is relational. It involves a multitude of relationships, in fact, the primary of which is between God and the worshiping assembly. But relationships abound between those who gather for worship: between the presider and the assembly, among those leading worship, and, of course, between the community and the Word. As St. Paul reminds us, it is through this final relationship that faith is called into being.

As Lutheran Christians, we understand that the constitutive Word can be either experienced through proclamation or sacramentally. Robert Jenson refers to baptism and the Eucharist as *visible words* in his book by the same name.[1] The way in which the sacramental words *speak* is through their Spirit-filled communication of God's grace in the assembly's worship. Just as a spoken word offers the community an audible dialogue with God, so the sacraments of baptism and Eucharist offer the community, and every person in it, a visible relationship with our Creator, Redeemer, and Sustainer.

Both Word and Sacrament are means of grace by which God calls us to faith, sustains faith, and empowers faith for witness in the world. So we worship: gathering to praise such a good and gracious God, to receive and be nurtured by the gifts of our God by hearing, eating, and drinking, and to be sent into the world to live our faith.

Beyond these liturgical relationships, however, the catechumenate offers a one-to-one relationship between a person coming to faith and his or her sponsor. The sponsor or mentor is a person who walks side by side, one to one with the Christian-in-formation over that one-year period of our catechumenal process.

---

1. Jenson, *Visible Words.*

A characteristic of The WAY previously mentioned is that there is no curriculum. We have come to say that our curriculum is lectionary and life. What we mean by that is that every person—inquirer, new convert, or lifelong disciple—comes to the Scriptures with his or her own set of life experiences. *What does this mean?* The agonies and ecstasies of everyday living provide rich and abundant grist for discussion, enrichment, and interaction with the Word of God. This interaction allows for new and longtime Christian alike to listen for the voice of the Holy Spirit to lead and guide them. The WAY helps all God's people to see the Spirit's breath blowing through their vocations, in marriage, in parenting, in sickness, in triumph, in every aspect of life, challenging or joyous.

The catechumenate: *what does this mean?* Foundationally, it means a way of being with one another and with our God that is dialogical, relational, and drawn from the deep wells of the participants' real-life experiences and interactions with the Holy Scriptures. Kathryn came because she hoped to find healing in a time of deep grief. Harrison came because he wanted to die in relationship to Christ and the Church, not alienated as he had been for much of his adult life. Kevin came because his wife's witness to the faith encouraged him to desire a similar experience with the God who had created and redeemed him. None of them could have told you when they arrived at our door *what* they were seeking. They simply knew that they were *seeking.* By the grace of God and the wise planning of those who had gone before them in the faith in this place, we were prepared to respond. There was a rattling in our bones and we had come to life—a life in Christ that we were prepared and eager to share with others.

Once, when leading a catechumenal training event for a congregation in another state, I heard from them a familiar refrain. It went something like this: "You come from a big city church in a highly unchurched area of the country. We just don't have unchurched people visiting our congregation like you do." I preached at Sunday worship during the weekend of that training event. As I was shaking hands in the narthex, a young couple with a lovely daughter in a car seat thanked me for the sermon and the visit to their parish. "Has your daughter been baptized yet?" I asked them. They were so delighted to tell me that she had, just a few weeks prior. This was her husband's church, the young mother told me, and it obviously meant a great deal that the place where he had grown up, and where the couple had married, was now the place where their daughter would worship, go to Sunday School, and grow among Christian friends. "And what about you?" I asked her.

"I've never been baptized. I never even went to church until I met Ray."

"Would you like to be baptized?"

"Of course!" she beamed.

"So why weren't you baptized with your daughter?"

"I didn't know you could do that. Before this very moment, no one ever asked me if I'd ever been baptized."

In the course of a three-minute conversation, I had unearthed a candidate for baptism who had been in the life of this congregation for at least two or three years. Yet the leaders were convinced that they didn't have any candidates within reach. Why? *No one ever asked me.*

As our nation—our cities, towns, and congregations—becomes further and further removed from a mythical time in American history when "everyone was Christian," it becomes more and more important for us to give clear, abundant, and invitational opportunities to those among us who have not had the gift of Christianity in their families for generations. *What does this mean?* It means seizing the opportunity to lay out before an unchurched, seeking population the series of welcome mats that the catechumenate's ministry provides. This model deserves consideration and prayerful study in every congregation, whether large or small. To bring men and women to the waters of baptism is both a mandate and a privilege to which our Lord invites us. Having a process of welcome in place allows God's people to provide for those who have not yet heard and known the wonders that the Lord has done for us. It is the Spirit's breath reviving dry bones in a desert of human longing for meaning and purpose.

What does this mean? It means that every congregation understands itself as a center for mission. It means that we live in a spirit of expectation that God can and will use congregations like ours to draw men, women, and children to life in Christ. It means that as faithful disciples of Christ, we are called to be open, welcoming, hospitable, and *ready* to share with an increasingly needy world the good news of Jesus Christ. Ours is the privilege of pointing people away from themselves, and all the things of the world that bring death, and to point them instead to the source of life and hope. Ours is the call to introduce women and men of our generation to a life of service to others in a needy, aching world. This is the birthright of the baptized people of God.

6

The Baptismal Shift

From Personal Demand to Relational Responsibility

WHEN DON MAIER ARRIVED in Seattle to begin his ministry in 1989, there were over two hundred children under
the age of eighteen on the roster of the congregation of Phinney
Ridge Lutheran Church whom no one in leadership knew. Many
of their baptisms had taken place privately, either in homes or at
specially arranged services at church, but with only the family
attending. The children were baptized simply because parents,
grandparents, or friends asked to have them baptized. Among
Protestants in the seventies and eighties, there was still enough
of a Christian ethos lingering even among inactive members to
make baptism all but required. For parents or relatives who had
even the most tangential connection to a community of faith, the
act of baptism was equated with salvation, but not necessarily with
ongoing life in Christ through the ministry of the Church. When
one couples that with the state church mentality of Christians
whose roots are in Scandinavia and northern Europe, for whom
the expectation of a service-providing church (baptize/confirm/
marry/bury) were deeply ingrained, one can imagine the pattern.
That pattern led to two decades of children who had received the
gift of baptism freely, but whose parents, sponsors, and congregation were never opened to the possibilities, privileges, and joys
of baptismal commitment. There was only gift, no responsibility.

As with other paradigm shifts, liturgical and theological shifts tend to take place subtly over time. It wasn't until a new pastor arrived that the congregation began to understand that while many children had been added to the roster, the strength of their Christian community had been diminished, not enhanced, by these baptisms. One of the central promises that parents make for their children at the time of baptism in the Lutheran tradition is "to teach their children the Creed, the Lord's Prayer, and the Ten Commandments." It is safe to venture that the vast majority of the parents who brought their children during these years didn't fully know these treasures of the faith for themselves. If they did know the words, they hadn't been offered the opportunity for serious theological reflection on what the words meant.

If anyone was at fault for the many ways in which baptismal preparations were nonexistent, it was the church's leadership, not the parents and well-meaning family members. The latter were doing what they thought the faith asked of them: to bring their children into God's house. That was what their parents had done with them, and their grandparents had done the generation before. What the Church failed to notice was that no one understood the significance of baptism, nor the reasons why a child might be brought to the font. In many cases it was the way things were done, a family tradition, and even if parents brought children under duress to maintain extended family peace, there was at least the good feeling that one's child was eternally "protected."

It's always more healthy and productive to imagine how things might be better than to assign blame for the way things are. So the congregation set out with Pastor Maier's leadership to do just that. Even though the end of baptism on demand would still be years in the distance, the first steps of educating parish leadership about the sheer numbers of children for whom the congregation had failed any sort of pre- or post-baptismal ministry were convincing. Parish-wide worship and educational materials, Bible studies, sermons, and rituals began to demonstrate the centrality and blessing of the sacrament of baptism in our theology and help people interpret *both* its gifts and responsibilities in a more serious light. Phinney Ridge was following the lead of its denomination, whose worship resource at the time, *The Lutheran Book of Worship,* said of baptism's importance and centrality: "[one goal of this resources is] to restore to Holy Baptism the liturgical rank and dignity implied by Lutheran theology, and to draw out the baptismal motifs in such acts as the confession of sin and the burial of the dead."[1]

Fast-forward to 2010, almost two decades later. In the fifteen years of my ministry, which began in 1995, only with rare exception has there been a baptism that has taken place apart from the regular worshiping community. Parents like Robert and Maria who bring their first child for baptism become candidates in The WAY where, along with others exploring the Christian faith, they can see what baptism means for them, not just for their children. What does my child's baptism mean *for me?* is a central question that we assist parents to consider as they themselves prepare to affirm their baptism. In some cases, such as with Kevin, the preparation for his own baptism and that of his child are taking place simultaneously.

As is widely practiced with premarital counseling, there is now a paradigm for pre-baptismal counseling. In fact, I often use the following example with parents as I visit with them about the baptism of their children. "Just as you prepared to stand before the altar and promise your lives to one another, the congregation and I want to assist you as you prepare to stand before the altar and offer your child to God." These are some of the most significant decisions and promises that parents will ever make for their children, and it is certainly incumbent upon us as leaders in Christ's Church to be forthright, honest, and thorough with our brothers and sisters in Christ about what these promises entail.

Placing in their hands the Holy Scriptures, another of the promises of our liturgy for baptism, means more than giving their child a children's Bible on the day of his or her baptism and

1. *The Lutheran Book of Worship,* 8.

having it on the shelf until they return twelve years later to begin confirmation instruction. Parents deserve to know what Christ and Christ's Church expect as they present their children for this powerful, life-changing sacramental gift. And more importantly, parents deserve to learn the many ways in which the community of faith is there to support them in the formational journeys on which they are embarking as parents of newly baptized children.

In what many present-day practitioners of the catechumenate regard as the very first catechumenal story of the New Testament, Philip encounters an Ethiopian diplomat on the desert road between Jerusalem and Gaza. The nameless Ethiopian is a seeker, reading without understanding from the prophecy of Isaiah when Philip comes upon him. Philip asks, "Do you understand what you are reading?" and the Ethiopian replies, "How can I, unless some one guides me?" (Acts 8:30–31).

This brief but powerful encounter has resounded through the ages as a testimony to the importance of interpreting to those who are seeking just what it is that life in Christ has to offer. This is the gift and responsibility of parish leadership. In an unchurched culture, one that is becoming more so every day, we cannot simply assume that everyone knows.

Anyone with pastoral experience will no doubt quickly arrive in their own imaginations at the last stop of the train of protest. It is this: "You mean that you are going to *deny* my child the gift of baptism because of your program?" Frankly, it's a protest we hear in one form or another not only from parents, grandparents, and friends, but also from colleagues as we move around the church to preach and teach about the catechumenate. The collegial response is more nuanced: "Baptism is a sacrament of grace. How can you possibly put any sort of conditions on those who are seeking it?"

Careful, prayerful, pastoral conversation is always the key in helping people make the shift to a new way of understanding and practicing baptismal ministry. These are not conditions, they are opportunities. We are not laying out demands, we are offering assistance. We are not trying to make baptism an elite opportunity for a chosen few; rather, we are attempting to open its treasures fully to all. With these sorts of convictions and expectations as the starting point of the conversation, the skilled and caring pastor can then begin to enter into a conversation with a parent or parents about the particularities of their own circumstances and needs. It has been our experience in over fifteen years of catechumenal practice that as parents and parish come to see and understand just how seriously the commitments and gifts of baptism are considered, they are persuaded that the time, effort, and energy that goes into preparing thoughtfully for this most important of parenting responsibilities is well worth their participation. (See Appendix 1.) It is this care and thorough education around both baptism's gifts *and* its call to discipleship that builds a church for mission. It transforms the question of an egocentric generation from "What does baptism mean for me?" into "How does baptism initiate me into a life of service and compassion for others?" If the former is the only question upon which we are focused, is it any wonder that baptism is seen as a single moment in time in which each recipient of the sacrament becomes eternally cared for? When baptism is broadened to include that salvific gift *and* all of the disciplines that following Jesus offers us as Christians, then baptism becomes a life-giving, lifelong journey of discovery. *What does this mean?* How can I best serve the Lord Jesus who first reached out to me and made me God's own child?

7

Parish Transformation

WHEN THE ADULT CATECHUMENATE was initiated in our congregation, no one could have imagined the impact that it would have on the life of the parish fifteen years later. Specifically, we could not have predicted what would happen to *us*—that is, to the people who were already present in the life of the congregation, fully engaged and walking a particular pathway in our life together in Christ. Despite its significant decline in membership between the 1960s and the mid-1990s, Phinney Ridge was and always has been a healthy and mission-minded congregation. But the catechumenate began to organize our lives in a specific and focused way and did, in fact, lead to surprising manifestations of God's grace among us that were brought about by changes both individual and corporate.

Imagine the life of any parish as a wheel with many spokes. A hub that connects those spokes is either consciously chosen by a healthy congregation or inflicted by circumstances in a less-than-healthy one. For some congregations, the hub is social justice. All of its educational ministries are interpreted through the hub of its social ministries. Its worship, preaching, and sacramental life are interpreted through social justice concerns as well. For another parish, liturgical life or a music program might be the hub. In dysfunctional parishes, it could even be a controlling family or group that serves as the connective tissue through which all other tendons, muscles, and nerves are connected.

For us, certainly after fifteen years of its practice, the cate-chumenate has become the lens through which all of parish life is viewed. To be more specific, it is not the *program* of The WAY, but the *process* of the annual cycle of bringing people to the waters of baptism and beyond that influences all congregational activities. We are a parish about faith forming faith. Our faith is forming faith in others, and their faith forms deeper faith in us. Because we are forming new Christians in the faith of Jesus Christ, when we are at our best we are constantly asking ourselves the ques-tion, How does *this* (fill in the blank) form us in faith *together*? The blank could be almost anything. How does this *Bible study,* this *sermon,* this *liturgy,* this *web page,* this *outreach ministry,* this *stewardship decision* form us in faith as a people of the living Lord Jesus Christ?

The catechumenate has taught us that forming faith forms *us.* Bringing men, women, and children to the waters of baptism and beyond, or intentionally reengaging people who have been away from the church for a few years or a lifetime, is a transfor-mational gift of God in their lives and in the life of the congre-gation. We are also formed in faith as we do our best to follow God's invitation to bring the Gospel to a world in need. The work of forming new Christians forms "old" Christians as well. The Gospel not only reaches others through us, but we who offer our-selves in loving support of those exploring the faith of Christ for the first time find that our faith is challenged, deepened, formed, and re-formed as well.

Dorothy Tuvey, an eighty-year-old woman who walked side by side with a much younger woman and served as the younger woman's sponsor, said, "I have held just about every office in the church, served in every capacity over the eighty years since I was baptized into the Christian faith in this congregation in 1921. But I have never done anything as spiritually enriching as this."

Dot speaks for just about everyone who has had the experi-ence of serving as a sponsor for a candidate for baptism or affir-mation of baptism. One simply cannot make that journey over the period of a year with any sort of integrity and not have it change *them*. The one who sponsors as well as the one who is being sponsored is formed in faith. To sit knee to knee with new Christians; to hear their struggles or share in their joys; to pray with them, study Scripture with them, worship with them week in and week out; to become their companion in the faith is an awesome and life-changing experience. It puts faith formation at the hub of one's individual life in the same way that the practice of the catechumenate places it at the center for the parish at large.

Many of the changes in parish life were unintentional. We simply looked around one day and noticed, as a result of investing so much time and energy in responding to God's call to reach others with the Gospel, that changes had occurred. Worship attendance increased as the unquestioned importance of the proclaimed Word of God moved to the center. There were more of us at worship week in and week out. Having an intentional process for welcoming and receiving those who inquire into the faith generates visitors who come back, knowing that their inquiries are taken seriously. We became friendlier, more open, and vulnerable to one another's needs. This is certainly the result of the small group Bible study component of The WAY. When questions are cherished and honored in small groups, little by little the larger assembly becomes a safe place to explore all aspects of faith, even doubt. Kathryn's truth-telling at the congregational forum was empowered by the truth that she told and the truths she was told by her small group as she prepared for her baptism.

Other changes were more intentional. The organizational model of the parish shifted from committee to task force. Those committees that were serving an obsolete or outdated function were simply left to dissolve, with the blessing of staff and lay leaders. At one time the parish had an active and robust fellowship committee that organized, reported on, and oversaw social activities for the entire parish as well as individualized age groups within the congregation. As times changed and more and more people became absorbed into leadership roles in The WAY, the committee floundered. In the end, leadership simply let the committee disband, realizing that, on the one hand, the process of the catechumenate was meeting many social needs within the congregation and, on the other hand, the need for a highly organized, regimented, and programmatic menu of fellowship activities was no longer desirable. Other priorities were taking precedence. Now when a need for a specific fellowship activity is perceived, those perceiving it are invited to form a task force, plan and carry out the activity, and then disband.

Much the same could be said about similar organizational structures and methods in educational, social ministry, and support ministries. We have come to realize the committee structure can often be life-sapping rather than life-giving. Faith formation is more important. This short, poignant poem by Ann Weems from her collection *Kneeling in Jerusalem* summarizes well our evolving insights.

> *Forgive, O Holy One*
>
> Stressed and anxious,
> the people come
> to be comforted
> and are put into committee.
> Forgive, O Holy One,
> our weariness
> with your world
> and with your word.[1]

Bible study that is thoughtful, well planned, largely clergy-led, and highly academic is a parish staple. We wish there were more hours in the week for this. People clearly hunger for it. Avoided at all costs are the sorts of Bible studies that give simplistic or pat responses. The catechumenate has taught us that the voice of the Holy Spirit speaks powerfully through *all* God's people and that insights brought to us by those who are questioning the faith are often exactly the sorts of questions that propel all of us to a new plateau of understanding.

1. Weems, *Kneeling in Jerusalem*, 37.

As part of her research for *Christianity for the Rest of Us,* Diana Butler Bass made this observation about the depth of educational life at Phinney Ridge:

> On a lovely Sunday morning in May, a dozen people gather for the pastor's Bible study class at Phinney Ridge Lutheran Church in Seattle. They sit at a round table with their Bibles open. At the center of the table, a candle is burning. It smells of incense and serves as a gentle reminder that this is more than a classroom. God is in our midst; we are in sacred study. In addition to their Bibles, most people have three or four theology books stacked at their elbows. The books are highlighted, and several have Post-it notes marking select passages. I recognize the books—they are substantial texts. I have required all of them for college classes I have taught over the years. The topic today is the problem of suffering.[2]

Looking around the Congregational Council table at most any meeting one will observe a vast majority of our leaders to be past or present participants in The WAY. Over the past fifteen years they have been candidates themselves who have recently been baptized or affirmed their baptism, or they have served as sponsors, or they have led in Sunday evening gatherings as catechists. Accordingly, there is no lack or appreciation among our leaders for the work and power of the Holy Spirit at the center of all of parish life, from the conduct of worship to fixing the roof. Meetings begin with clergy-led devotions and end with lay-led shared prayer for the concerns of the members and the parish. We have come to believe that it is often the newer, smaller voice that carries in its courageous question the guidance and direction of the Holy Spirit. Therefore, we have abandoned Robert's Rules of Order as our method of governance, which often results in winners and losers, and moved to the model of consensus where we come over time to lead with a common voice. We turned to the neighboring Mennonite parish to be taught the consensus

---

2. Bass, *Christianity for the Rest of Us,* 196.

style and were blessed by great insights, wonderful materials, and new friends.

Overall, we believe that we have come to be a more faithful congregation than we would have been without The WAY. We are known as a place that encourages questions and is a safe congregation in which to express both doubts and fears.

Being a congregation of the catechumenate has also changed the way we pray. Because candidates and sponsors pray with and for one another in the time of baptismal preparation, the expectation of prayer pervades all of parish life. No meeting, large or small, begins or ends without prayer. Parishioners are encouraged in their daily prayer life to pray for those in need—both those listed on the weekly bulletin's prayer list and those known only to God. A regular feature of our weekly liturgical prayers is the request that God continue to send men, women, and children to our congregation that they may be welcomed into the faith through our ministry. A simple, repeated ritual is one of the last things that happens each year as all the candidates and sponsors gather for the Easter Vigil. Before we join the rest of the congregation to begin the service, we invite the group to look around the room at one another, and we remind them that each of them is an answer to our prayers: "We prayed for you to come, and God has sent you to us. We are so grateful for you. This is the night we have waited for. You are the people God sent to us."

There is a culture of expectation that living together under the cross of Christ creates. It is a culture that is often missing in other parishes to which we have been invited to teach, or into which we have been called to observe and assist. After leading a Bible study among a group of Council members in a Midwestern Lutheran congregation, I invited them to close the study by joining in prayer, praying particularly for the person seated to their right. When the circle of prayer concluded, one of the members dared to speak what was on everyone's mind, saying, "This is the first time we have ever prayed for each other." On more occasions than anyone would care to count, in workshops that pastors and lay leaders from our congregation have led, the participants respond with something like this: "We understand the need to bring others into the family of God in our congregation. We just don't feel like we have anything appealing to bring them *to.*"

The willingness to accept that paradigm shift to a culture of expectation is primary. Before considering beginning the cat-echumenate in one's congregation, the best question that a parish could consider is, Are we prepared to welcome and expect that awesome, amazing grace of God that the newly baptized will surely bring us? In other words, will we recognize and welcome the unexpected presence of God's grace when it appears?

8

Creating a Climate of Expectation

A SURPRISING VISITOR

ONE NIGHT SHORTLY BEFORE Christmas, the unexpected appeared on our doorstep. It was a little after seven on a Wednesday evening and, as is always the case at that day and time, the elementary and middle school children of the parish were gathered on the steps for closing worship after an evening of music, education, and a shared meal that we call Bread for the Journey. The closing worship at Bread for the Journey is brief and simple. The sixty or so kids gather on the steps, joined by some of their parents and all of their teachers. Older kids embrace the younger ones and invite them to sit beside them or on their laps. It's already been a long day at school and a long evening at church, and everyone is pretty tired. We sing the opening service of light from Evening Prayer, hear the Gospel story for the coming week told at a child's level, sing, pray, and are dismissed with a benediction offered by one of the children themselves.

The Bible story on this particular evening was from Matthew 25. It was the parable of the five wise and five foolish bridesmaids who went to the wedding feast, the former with plenty of oil, the latter with none at all. The five unprepared women, after trying unsuccessfully to get oil from the wise, must go off to purchase their own, and when they return, the door to the wedding feast is locked; although they knock, they cannot get in. Just as I got to that part of the story, the most amazing thing happened: There was a tremendous knock at the church door, the one closest to where the children were gathered. Even I was astonished, thinking that one of the other leaders had put someone up to this. The adults present for worship were sure that it was I who had planned the real-life interruption in the story. But it was neither. It was simply a knock. When I walked to the door and answered it, I could hardly believe my eyes. It was a homeless person thinking that they were knocking at the door of our Food Bank. The Food Bank had opened at seven o'clock as well, just as our worship was beginning.

In other circumstances, I might have simply directed the woman to the Food Bank, closed the door, and continued leading worship. But sixty young children of God are a company of great expectation, and they wanted to know how the story was going to end. Not just that Bible story; they wanted to know how *this* story was going to end. What was God going to do in their lives? In the life of this woman? In our shared lives? Would she be turned away because she did not have what was required, or welcomed to join us in the loving praise and worship of a living, surprising, gracious God?

It was one of those moments when the Holy Spirit was truly at work and leading us. I simply can't think that fast. But I knew from somewhere deep in our shared culture of expectation that the thing to do was to invite this homeless, hungry child of God to have a place among us, worship with us, pray with us, and then find what she had come looking for—a week's supply of food. It's a lesson in the Living Word that none of us who were present will ever forget. God was at work, and we could recognize God at work among us because we expected God to be at work among us.

It is the responsibility of the clergy and parish leaders to create a culture of expectation. In a world that is fully saturated with mind-numbing media, parishioners old and young alike are used to having their interpreting done for them. Commercials tell them what to think about consumer products or political candidates, search engines direct them to resources, smart phones put endless resources in reach within seconds, and sitcoms dictate emotional responses. In all things theological, thoughtful and insightful responses are even more difficult to come by and therefore less readily available to the members of our worshiping communities.

What a joyful responsibility of the ordained to have this ministry of the Gospel—to help point the way to the signs of God's love and grace that surround us every day. Giving *an* interpretation rather than *the* interpretation will ignite the faith of others to bring their own experiences of God into the open as a way of witnessing to others both inside and outside the community of faith and strengthening the faith of the entire community. Here are some examples taken from our congregation's recent ministry.

GOD'S SECRETS

The youngest formally organized liturgical choir of the parish meets weekly for a half-hour rehearsal and faith formation time. Each session concludes with a five-minute devotional rite in which candles appropriately colored and decorated for the liturgical season are lit and prayers by the kindergarten, first and second graders are offered. Recently, the choir learned a stanza of the hymn "O Master Let Me Walk with You" for leadership in parish worship. Many readers will recall that a portion of the hymn's text refers to God's secret: "Tell me your secret / help me bear the strain of toil, the fret of care." As a part of the closing, their leader asked the children to think about God's secrets. Here is a sampling of the responses, offered in prayer:

"I think God's secret is how he made the world out of nothing."

"God's secret is how he watches everything all the time."

"I want to know the secret of where God was before he created the world."

"How can God love all of us?"

These responses were not prompted. They all came from the minds and lips of the children, and they gave witness to a deep and abiding faith. They were offered because their questions were expected and honored, and over time, the children came to recognize this closing devotional time as a safe and welcoming place to experiment with and in which to offer their developing theological reflections.

A GESTURE OF BLESSING FOR ALL

Another incident of expectation involved a confirmation class of eighth graders. At preparatory rehearsal for the rite, we came to the part in the liturgy where the congregation prays its prayer of blessing over the new affirmers. "So this is where the congregation will all raise their hands in blessing over us, right?" one of the girls piped up. "Well, we don't actually have them raise their hands at confirmation. We just do that at the Easter Vigil for the newly baptized and the affirmers," I responded. "Why?" she challenged.

Why, indeed! She was exactly right to raise the issue. Year after year, she had watched at the vigil as the congregation joined in a gesture of solidarity and blessing over the newly affirmed and had anticipated the day when she and her classmates would be the recipients of such an act of grace. The rites were identical, and it was not only appropriate but important that she and her classmates receive this gift as well. Needless to say, the congregation has raised its hands in blessing at every confirmation liturgy since.

"I KNOW NOW WHAT THOSE WORDS MEAN"

"O come, O come Emmanuel / and ransom captive Israel / that mourns in lonely exile here / until the Son of God appear."

Familiar Advent words to most any Christian, young or old. One might not think of them as kid-friendly words, but they are certainly words that kids can manage, and throughout their worship and choral experiences at church, our young people have taken these words into their heads and hearts.

During an Advent season several years ago, some of the parish's young women had a schoolmate who committed suicide. In order to reach out and comfort them, one of the choral directors who knew both our girls and the one who had died invited the girls to stay for a special prayer together following the usual Bread for the Journey closing worship. They gathered together around the font, prayed for Jessica and her family, and sang "O Come, O Come, Emmanuel." As the girls were walking out together, one of them said to the director, "I guess I know now what those words mean."

"Which words?"

"Mourn in lonely exile here," she replied, through her tears.

The words were planted in young hearts with the full expectation that one day they might ripen and bear fruit in a more mature life and thereby bring comfort and hope. It was an expectation that God did not disappoint.

GROWING INTO FAITH

A young member of our parish, upon his own affirmation of baptism—what many congregations would typically call confirmation—wrote the following statement of faith in preparation for this important day in his life. Preparing such a statement is standard practice in our parish; it is part of what we all expect to see on that day, and we look forward to the posting of these statements with great anticipation.

Reier's statement is offered here because of its depth of understanding about faith as a continuing, lifelong process. He chose to connect his faith to Micah 6:8[1] and to give witness to

1. "He has told you, O mortal, what is good; and what does the Lord require of you but to do justice, and to love kindness, and to walk humbly with your God?"

an expectation of his own future growth and development that is wise beyond his thirteen years.

> As I think about my faith more, preparing for Affirmation of my Baptism, I realize that I am glad that my parents chose to baptize me when I was born. Because as I grow up and learn more about God, and the community that I take part in, I reach a greater understanding of something I will never fully understand, but I can grasp a stronger hold on it. This is something I may never have stumbled upon if my parents didn't choose to baptize me when I was young. Therefore I am confirming that I, by myself, choose to stay with God as I grow up and learn more about the world and make choices.
>
> —Reier Jacob VanSanford, October 31, 2010

AN UNCONDITIONAL EXPECTATION

One summer several years ago at the closing picnic of The WAY, one of the catechists was holding court with three or four young couples who had just completed the past year's cycle. "Why did you do it?" she asked them. "Why did you take this time out of your busy lives and come to the church every Sunday evening to study, learn, and pray together? What made you do it?" The responses were identical. "When the pastor visited us and told us about The WAY, there was an unconditional expectation that this is what we would do."

The climate of expectation that is embodied by The WAY in parish life carries over into our lives of worship, prayer, education, fellowship, and service. It is all about being formed together in faith. We all live in the hope and expectation that God is active among us and that at any moment, through the gift of one another and our shared lives, we will have the joy of knowing God revealed to us. We live in this hope, and this hope does not disappoint us.

9

The Great Vigil of Easter

IN PRECEDING CHAPTERS, MANY references have been made to the Easter Vigil. Here we turn our attention to this magnificent, ancient service of the church, centered in baptism and revived among postmodern Christians as the pinnacle of the Church Year. An ancient homily, the preacher of which is unidentified, hints at the breadth and magnificence of this night in the life of the Church:

> Something strange is happening—there is a great silence on earth today, a great silence and stillness. The whole earth keeps silence because the King is asleep. The earth trembled and is still because God has fallen asleep in the flesh and he has raised up all who have slept ever since the world began. God has died in the flesh and hell trembles with fear . . . I am your God, who for your sake have become your son. See on my face the spittle I received in order to restore to you the life I once breathed into you. See the marks of the blows I received in order to refashion your warped nature in my image. On my back see the marks of the scourging I endured to remove the burden of sin that weighs upon your back. See my hands, nailed firmly to a tree, for you who once wickedly stretched out your hand to a tree. I slept on the cross and a sword pierced my side for you who slept in paradise and brought forth Eve from your side. My side has healed the pain in yours. My sleep will rouse you from your sleep in hell. The sword that pierced me has sheathed the

sword that was turned against you. The bridal chamber is adorned, the banquet is ready, the eternal dwelling places are prepared, the treasure houses of all good things lie open. The kingdom of heaven has been prepared for you from all eternity.[1]

An Easter Vigil is better experienced than described. It is a night when God's people recall what only God can do. It is poetic, dramatic, a time in which the story of salvation unfolds. One of its major liturgical pieces, the Exsultet, is attributed to Hippolytus from the third century. Christians since then have joined their voices and sung it as the Easter light is spread throughout the darkened church, describing the vigil in this way:

This is the night when Christians everywhere,
washed clean of sin and freed from all defilement,
are restored to grace and grow together in holiness.[2]

Attending a vigil on the Saturday night before Easter at a neighboring congregation, regardless of denomination, on a seminary campus, or at a time other than Holy Week at a catechumenal training event is by far the best way to become familiar with its wonders. Nevertheless, from the perspective of one particular congregation in one particular denomination, the following description will help the reader better see and more fully appreciate the experiences that have inspired us and by which we have been fed for the past twenty Easter seasons.

The vigil stands historically as the night of great mystery in the life of Christ, marking his Passover from death into life. The Church borrows from the story of the Hebrews fleeing slavery in Egypt the idea of *pascha*, or passage. Built on this first Passover, the vigil emphasizes a host of passages that constitute Christian life: death to life, slavery to freedom, sin to forgiveness, darkness to light. Every element of the vigil in some way surrounds the

1. Huck and Simcoe, "From an Ancient Homily," in *Triduum Sourcebook*, 65.

2. Huck and Simcoe, "Exsultet," in *Triduum Sourcebook*, 76.

community of faith with the stories, sights, sounds, smells, and sensations of a living, risen Christ among us. It is this Christ who invites those prepared for baptism into the waters where the old life will be put to death and a new life in Christ will be resurrected. This pattern of baptismal dying and rising, grounded in Romans 6, becomes the pattern for all Christians in their daily lives. The vigil has four parts—four distinct services for the Eve of Easter—and each gives witness to many aspects of Christ's gracious gift of saving passages in our lives. Each gives the community of faith the opportunity to worship and praise God for Christ's Easter gift of new, resurrected life, a gift for all eternity.

- Service of Light
- Service of Readings
- Service of Holy Baptism
- Service of Holy Communion

The congregation gathers in silence, preferably at a location outdoors and completely separated from its usual place of worship. A fire pit is prepared into which a new fire will be struck. As the Service of Light progresses, the new fire is passed to the paschal candle from which all worshipers will light their own handheld candles once they enter the darkened church. The presider's words at the fire recall creation, with its motifs of darkness turning to light at the powerful hand of the Creator. They further remind the community that this is the night of the New Creation, connecting Jesus' resurrection to the pattern of creation itself. Following the paschal candle, lit from the new fire, the congregation accompanies the ministers into the darkened church. Like Israelites following the pillar of fire so long ago, we follow the liturgical equivalent of that pillar of fire, the paschal candle, on our mysterious Easter journey from darkness to light, from slavery to freedom, from death to life.

Once gathered inside the church, all of these passages are further revealed to the congregation. Various ways of retelling the story of Christ's *pascha* are available in every denomination and parish, but as that story is told or sung, the individual candles of worshipers are lit. The darkness of the "empty tomb" begins to brighten with the hope of the light of Christ.

Thus bathed in shared light, the congregation settles in to hear and be renewed in the formative stories of God's saving grace from the Old Testament. Twelve readings are appointed for the vigil, all with deep, historic liturgical roots and all containing some element of the motif of *pascha*, passage. We've learned over the years to vary the styles of reading and the congregation's responses to the readings. Seldom do congregations read all twelve texts. We begin our vigil early in the evening in order to be able to include the parish's children. We also limit the number of readings to six or seven so as to accommodate the listening limits of those in the elementary school years.

As the service of readings concludes, a hymn is sung or a scriptural song is chanted, the church is fully bathed in light, the baptismal font revealed, and the candidates gather around the waters of new life. As The WAY has progressed, we have used the language and the story of the Red Sea to help new Christians make the connections between the ancient Jewish Passover and Christ, the new Passover lamb. When the vigil is taught and rehearsed among the candidates, we refer to the font as our congregation's "local Red Sea" to assist in their comprehension of God's continuing saving grace. Just as God led the people of Israel out of slavery in Egypt at the hand of Moses, so God now leads us out of our old life of sin into a new life of forgiveness and hope at the hand of Christ.

The baptisms are celebrated with great joy and flourish. A large, portable tub that will accommodate children and adults for full immersion is used. Members of the congregation are invited prior to the baptisms to participate in a water procession. Through this action, everyone who desires to do so is encouraged to come forward with a container of his or her own choosing to pour water into the font in preparation for receiving new brothers and sisters into the community. Emphasizing baptism's connection to vocation and daily life, we encourage the water carriers to use containers that have special meaning or purpose in their lives or that are in some way connected to their vocation. Baptism belongs to all God's people. It is an act of the community receiving new members, not a private ceremony between a pastor and a candidate. Members of the congregation sing, clap, shout praises, weep, and celebrate that God has brought new people into the family of faith among us.

As a part of our baptismal practice, we anoint not only the newly baptized but all those who desire to receive this sign of yet another passage on this most holy night. Anointing is a practice deeply rooted in the Old Testament; its language fills our baptismal liturgy, and its incorporation into the liturgy gives an added dimension of communal celebration and baptismal witness for every one of God's people, whether he or she has been a participant in this year's cycle of The WAY or not.

The liturgy reaches its peak with the climactic, life-giving Gospel of the resurrection of Christ being proclaimed. Thus begins the service of Holy Communion. Even with Easter morning's festival liturgy just ten or twelve hours away, we nonetheless feast together on the gifts of bread and wine, enjoying our first communion with the newest members of the community of Christ. They have waited so long for this moment, and we rejoice to share it with them.

Any parish can celebrate an Easter Vigil with joy and dignity. With worshipers gathered in an assembly that is large or small, highly liturgical or in a more casual style, the crowning service of the church's year in which all the wonder of Christ's death and resurrection are proclaimed and celebrated deserves the careful attention and consideration of every worshiping community. The ancient church has gifted us with the vigil as a model of baptismal theology, and every Christian's understanding of the scriptural connections between God's saving grace revealed in the Bible and his or her own life as a baptized child of God will be enhanced and strengthened through its celebration.

Kevin, following his baptism (the story of which I told in chapter 4), reflected that he had no idea how much it meant until he entered the darkened church on the night before Easter and saw all those people gathered for the celebration of his and his daughter's baptisms, along with that of many others and the affirmations of even more candidates with whom he had walked in The WAY. As the spreading candlelight brought increased intensity of the light of Christ among us, it also brought an intensity of desire in him to enter those saving waters and so to be reborn as a child of God.

In all of these things, the Spirit's breath was again blowing over the dry valley of ordinary lives in a desert called Seattle. By that breath, both the newly baptized and those whose lives have been grounded in Christ for years were brought refreshment and grace. Each year the vigil reminds us that through the death and resurrection of Christ, and by his gracious invitation to join him through the waters of baptism, we are passing from death to life. The Spirit's breath comes into us, and we shall live.

10

The Power of Passion Sunday Evening

THE GREAT VIGIL ON the night before Easter is clearly the
most powerful night of Holy Week for all who participate
in The WAY each year and for the entire congregation as well.
Beyond Saturday, it would be hard to choose which other night of
Holy Week is the *second* most important. Is it Maundy Thursday,
with its celebration of the institution of the Lord's Supper, foot
washing, and the stripping of the altar? Is it Good Friday, with
the solemn reading of St. John's Passion and the lighting of
candles around the cross? From the vantage point of leadership,
I would have to nominate the evening of Passion Sunday as the
most important to our welcoming process of faith formation for
the candidates. That might seem a strange choice, but read on.

Passion Sunday evening is the night of our rehearsal with all
the members of The WAY for the Easter Vigil service. In addition
to those candidates for baptism and affirmation of baptism that
have been a part of the process since the previous autumn, the
night also includes all those members of the community who are
bringing their children for the sacrament of baptism just six days
away.

While this rehearsal began years ago as a "blocking rehearsal," it has evolved through experience into one of the most significant teaching opportunities that we have in the entire WAY
experience. Certainly the blocking or logistical function of the
evening is important. Who goes where, and when, in a liturgy as

complicated as the vigil is important for everyone to learn. One of the most significant acts of hospitality that a pastor can extend to lay participants in worship is acquainting them with the basic movements that will be required, the words that will be spoken and shared, the gestures that will be involved, and the meanings that these actions carry. Offering the participants this gift of familiarity allows them the privilege to enter the worship more fully and to become fully involved in the service as it unfolds. Their minds can rest from logistical worries and attend to ritual mysteries as they take place throughout the service. With a service as complex, varied, and rich in meaning as the Easter Vigil, this is certainly important. Bear in mind that the candidates for baptism or affirmation of baptism are about to make significant commitments of faith and life. These are commitments toward which they have been building, planning, praying, and hoping throughout The WAY for months. The responsibility to free them of detailed anxieties that fill the mind of lay persons new to liturgical celebrations and assist them to focus on the meaning of this life-changing event in their lives is vital. That responsibility lies with the presider.

In our parish, we are usually moving a group of fifty to seventy persons to various places in the chancel during the Service of Baptism within the vigil. The preparation, prayers, washing, anointing, laying on of hands, and welcome all involve different gestures and liturgical signs: with water, with oil, and with candles, to name a few. But even with a single baptism in a smaller parish, the importance of acquainting the participants with what is to come cannot be overstated. This sort of preparation is simply an act of hospitality.

In our homes, if our guests are experiencing a new food, we graciously encourage them, "We just pick these ribs up with our hands. No forks allowed." When new friends are introduced at a gathering, the host opens the conversation: "Meg and Ryan just moved here from Baltimore. She's taken a job at the university teaching economics." The same sort of acquainting hospitality and welcome is what this time together on Passion Sunday evening is intended to provide. It makes the coming celebration all the more meaningful for everyone. Its opportunity to teach is immeasurable as well. The liturgical equivalents of "we eat these with our hands" range from the pedestrian—"You'll probably want to take off your glasses before being anointed"—to the more theologically rich: "The people will clap when you emerge from the baptismal waters. Their joy at your incorporation into life in Christ will be overwhelming for them."

As leaders, we have grown to realize over the years that the Spirit is powerfully at work in this hour and a half that we spend together. God has formed us to see that it is a perfect opportunity for further catechesis. At few other times in the life of the parish will persons be so primed to learn of and understand the rich messages of Scripture and tradition that are lived out in this liturgy. At no other time will the candidates have such a deep interest in learning not only *what* is about to happen to them, but also *why. What does this mean?*—the question that stands at the foundation of the Lutheran expression of the Christian faith—is pregnant with possibilities this night.

We find that our candidates are incredibly eager to embrace the detailed explanations of the vigil's many facets as we are explaining the much more mundane necessities of "stand here," "walk over there," "be ready with a towel then." Much of this we have learned from the candidates themselves, who have expressed their desire to know more about their faith in their questions and responses as this complex rehearsal unfolds. A few examples follow.

With the font taking central place in this baptismal festival, we take time to elaborate upon the baptismal water's connections to the Red Sea experience of God's people, the Israelites. While at the vigil the words of the liturgy and prayers are filled with allusions to the Exodus, it helps the candidates embrace those connections more fully when, at the rehearsal, the presider says, "Think of this font as our Red Sea. This candle is our pillar of fire. These waters will be parted with the sign of the cross that the presider stretches out during the baptismal prayer, just as Moses stretched out his hand at God's command to part the water leading from slavery to freedom. Our slavery is from all that we leave behind in the old life of sin. Our freedom is that which Christ graciously promises in baptismal living where we are free to serve the neighbor in need, unencumbered by preoccupation with our own salvation."

Each congregation's liturgical practice will be different, and theological understanding will vary from denomination to denomination. The point is not to offer a sacramental theology through these examples. Rather, the point is to offer a pastoral theology of caring for the community by interpreting the tradition, *whatever that tradition may be* within the framework of one's own liturgical and theological understanding. As leaders, the opportunity to thoroughly think and practice this catechesis in preparation for the vigil has also helped to shape our practice. For example, if we pray and teach about a flood of God's grace in the waters of baptism, will a font with only the most modest amount of water reinforce and teach along with us? Will a small cotton napkin after a baptismal washing offer grace, or would a large towel be a more theologically evocative and appropriate gift?

All that is said above assumes a careful, prayerful, detailed time of preparation for the presider, her assistants, and those in leadership. The vigil rehearsal is not the time for the presider to discover that there is not enough space in the chancel to celebrate the baptisms as we had hoped. Nor is it the time for those in leadership to familiarize themselves for the first time with the words and actions of this mysteriously beautiful liturgy. Preparations done in advance will communicate confidence, assurance, and the grace that stands at the very center of the sacrament of holy baptism and that every candidate deserves.

Over the years, as the rehearsal has prepared all of us for the renewal of our baptismal life in the Vigil of Easter, one of the most profound insights that has occurred to us is this: we are not only rehearsing for the vigil. We are rehearsing for *new life in Christ.*

An example will serve to illustrate. In the Lutheran baptismal liturgy from *Evangelical Lutheran Worship,* the candidates for baptism and its affirmation are asked to make several renunciations. One will suffice to demonstrate the teaching possibilities: *Do you renounce the ways of sin that draw you from God?*

Over the years, the parish's practice has evolved into responding in the following manner. First, the candidates themselves respond in concert, *I renounce them.* Next, the candidates, along with the entire WAY group, respond, *I renounce them.* And in quick succession the entire congregation joins in responding, *I renounce them.* Thus, with each of these responses, there is a growing voice of renunciation: *I renounce them.* ***I renounce them. I renounce them.*** Initially, the trifold renunciation was meant to mirror the trifold confession of the Triune God: Father, Son, and Holy Spirit.

This, of course, is explained to the candidates. But there is more. And the *more* is likely much more significant for the practice of their faith and discipleship in daily life than the theological explanation. So, at the Passion Sunday rehearsal, this is what we tell them: "At some point in the near or distant future, the power of sin that draws you from God is going to become very real, very present in your life. You may be tempted to cut corners at the office for the sake of the bottom line. You may find yourself called back in a seemingly irresistible way to an old addiction. Perhaps you will find yourself seduced into a relationship that violates your marriage covenant. Whatever the case may be, when that temptation lurks close at hand, as your pastors we want you to have ringing in your ears the growing voices of renunciation: *I renounce them.* ***I renounce them. I renounce them.***" In this way, we name the temptations that face us all, and in so naming, begin the process of robbing temptation of its power over us. But more, we *teach* the candidates and remind ourselves that as a part of the baptized community of Christ, we do not face temptation alone. Baptism places us in community, and it is the community voice that will accompany the newly baptized in their new journey of discipleship in a real world with real temptations. Baptism makes us different.

In what might otherwise be "only a logistical rehearsal," the wise pastoral leader is able to assist the newly baptized in these and many ways to claim the inheritance of their coming covenant, just six days ahead at the Easter Vigil. Moreover, those same liturgical and theological connections are made for all the sponsors, all the catechists, and all the active member baptismal families as well. Truth be told, we are even reinforcing them in our own lives as pastors who live real lives in a real world.

I renounce them. **I renounce them. *I renounce them.*** There is no one, lay or clergy, who could not benefit from being reminded that God's community goes with us into our everyday lives. This assurance and so many other liturgical connections assist the entire community in entering more fully into baptismal living as the first day of Holy Week draws to a close with the Easter Vigil rehearsal on Passion Sunday evening.

I I

The Gracious Gift of Flexibility

VIRGINIA BEGAN VISITING OUR parish on Easter Sunday. She came because a member bumped into her at a coffee shop a block away from the church, where Virginia asked, "You must be all dressed up for Easter. Where is your church?" Over lattés, the parishioner invited her to come to Easter worship and breakfast and Virginia, not a practicing Christian in her adult lifetime, has been back almost every Sunday since.

When I visited with her over that summer about signing up for The WAY in the coming autumn, she readily agreed. "There's only one problem I can see with all this," she told me. "I'm retired, you know, and I go to Arizona for the bulk of the winter. So I'm not quite sure how I'm going to be able to participate in the weekly gatherings and small group Bible studies that you're talking about."

"Is there a church nearby your winter home that you would be willing to attend?"

"Yes."

"Would you be willing to worship there?"

"Of course."

"Then I think we can work this out."

We assigned Virginia a sponsor of her own generation who, like she, was fluent with e-mail. Each Sunday afternoon, our faithful member sent off a report of the sermon from Sunday worship. Virginia responded with what she had heard at her church-away-from-church in Arizona, and the week was filled with an exchange of thoughts and ideas. The two held each other in prayer. Virginia came home early enough to be included in the intense preparations of Lent and affirmed her baptism at the Easter Vigil, exactly one liturgical year after that Spirit-led coffeehouse conversation.

Such arrangements can make miracles like this one happen if the catechumenate is seen as a process rather than a program. The flexible welcome that Virginia received has opened her to all sorts of parish leadership and involvement, even though she still spends about five months each year in the Sun Belt.

The Radford, the Hostetler, and the Doorenbos families all had sixth-grade boys. They had been visiting the congregation for some time, drawn there by many of their children's friends, who encouraged the kids to come. The parents followed. A moment of decision was arriving for each family as they contemplated whether or not the boys should be enrolled with their peers in confirmation class. During pastoral visits about this possibility with each family, the topic of The WAY was discussed, but each family had unique and pressing concerns that made a regular Sunday evening commitment difficult. "Let's get the boys started in confirmation this fall and see where God leads us," I counseled. By the beginning of the boys' eighth-grade year, the Spirit's work was not readily apparent. Nothing had changed among the six adults, and each of the boys was about to become a member of the congregation through affirmation of baptism before any of their parents did. Our wise Associate Pastor proposed a solution. Since the families were often at Wednesday evening Bread for the Journey anyway, why not set up a special small group of The WAY for the six of them with a lay catechist and prepare them for affirmation of baptism at the Feast of the Baptism of our Lord? Everyone agreed. The boys were confirmed in late October, and on the second Sunday of January the following year, the six adults and one younger sibling in each family were received into membership. Each of the three teenage boys presented his parents to the congregation and announced them prepared for membership in the body of Christ. It was a moving and memorable culminating liturgy for the entire congregation. It stands as yet another example of what is possible when the catechumenate is seen as a gift of flexibility, loving support, and welcome rather than a program that has to be completed in order to make membership possible.

Early on in the days of catechumenal practice at Phinney Ridge, we established a one-time small group for nonmember spouses. As the time of Lent and intense preparation drew near for our regular participants in The WAY, we imagined a group that would be open to spouses of active members who either had never been baptized or had never been given a specific invitation to become an affirmer of their long-latent faith. Letters were sent to every spouse in the congregation who was not on the membership role asking for a response of (*a*) interested in learning more; (*b*) not interested; or (*c*) don't ask again.

This was back in the day before e-mail became the preferred method of communication, so each letter included a prepaid postcard asking for the return response. Five men and one woman replied, indicating their interest to participate. A group was formed in addition to those already in progress. The spouses served as the sponsors and I led the small group acting as catechist. The stories that poured out of those small group conversations were phenomenal.

One spouse said, "I always wanted to become a part of the congregation, but no one ever asked me. We really didn't know how to go about it."

Another spouse recalled, "When I'd come on Christmas Eve or Easter, I always felt ashamed. It wasn't my fault that I'd never been baptized; my parents just never got around to it. When I was here with Jennie and the kids (who all were baptized and communing), I felt embarrassed. It was easier to just stay home."

One of the spouses told me privately that she regarded the letter to her nonmember husband as "the deal of the century" when it arrived. "I've always wanted Travis to become more a part of things here, but I knew the invitation had to come to him from someone other than me. I was also pretty sure that an entire year of The WAY was more than he would go for, given his past background as an active Christian and participant before we got married. But this was just perfect. Thanks for your flexibility, your openness, your care. Now this feels like church for the *entire* family."

That year at the Easter Vigil, along with all the other baptismal candidates and affirmers, five wives and one husband stood side by side with their spouses, hands on their shoulders in prayer and blessing as they were baptized into the fellowship of the Gospel or as they affirmed a faith that had been left behind somewhere along the way. Among the men and women of this small, tailored group, one man has served as an officer on the parish council, one member has taken significant leadership of an elderly women's auxiliary at a local nursing home, and one organizes the annual Easter Sunday breakfast every year. The man who was embarrassed that he had never been baptized turned to the church at the time of his brother's unexpected early death, reassuring his family that "my church will help us out. I know they will." His brother's memorial service was held at Phinney Ridge, bringing through our doors an entire community of people from Seattle who were unchurched. Together, they experienced the unconditional love and grace of Christ at the time of deepest need.

FLEXIBILITY CREATES A PLACE AMONG THE PEOPLE OF GOD

Bradford and Sally had two small children, Roy and Jack. They began The WAY when Sally was eight months pregnant with Jack, and things went pretty well with them and their small group as well as with their sponsors. But when Jack was born, things changed. He was an unusually fussy baby; The WAY clashed with

Roy's bedtime and Jack's feedings. Sally called one day and simply said, "We quit. It's just too much."

"I understand. Let's talk in a few days," I said.

After consulting with their sponsors, I was able to call back a few days later and offer an alternative to The WAY as they had come to know it so far. "How would you feel about having your sponsors pick up Sunday evening's dinner at church, come over and eat with you at your house, and help get the kids to bed? Then you can sit together with the Bible study texts everyone else is discussing at church. This way you won't lose what you've already gained and in a few more weeks when Easter comes you can have the boys baptized and affirm your own faith just as you had planned."

Needless to say, Bradford and Sally were overwhelmed by the offer. Their sponsors gained a new set of grandchildren, the church gained four new disciples of Christ, and Bradford, Sally, and the boys gained an eternal place among the people of God rather than being shut out by a system that couldn't be flexible enough to meet their very real, very legitimate, and very human set of circumstances.

One of the true blessings and gifts of catechumenal practice is its adaptability and flexibility to the particular circumstances within one's parish and to the special needs of those who participate in the annual walk toward baptism or its affirmation. With a creative imagination and a pastoral ear and eye tuned to the needs of both parish and Christian apprentice, there are few limits on what is possible in bringing people into the welcoming arms of a loving Christ.

12

The Role of Lay Leaders and Clergy in the Catechumenate

PROVIDING A PROCESS OF formal welcome and formation into congregational life is absolutely dependent on the committed leadership and vision of lay members of the congregation. Not only is it important for the congregation as a whole to grasp and embrace the vision of parish transformation that the catechumenate brings, it is also equally important to have committed laypersons who are willing to share their faith and their time in the specific roles of lay Bible study leaders and sponsors. Following the language of the ancient church's process, we call our lay leaders of small groups catechists. Those who walk alongside each inquirer can be known as sponsors or mentors; in some places, they are even referred to as faith companions. At Phinney Ridge, we call our companions sponsors. The flexibility of the catechumenate's approach allows each congregation to use nomenclature that they find appropriate and meaningful for the various roles.

In each of the roles—sponsor and catechist—we believe that a demonstrated example of commitment to the congregation's life of worship is primary among the characteristics for those chosen to serve. Without tangible evidence that those leading new Christians to the waters of baptism are persons who deeply embrace the church's central commitment to the worship and praise of our Creator, Redeemer, and Sustainer, the invitation offered to others of a life of discipleship rings hollow. It is also important that those serving in leadership roles espouse a spirit of welcome and theological flexibility and openness. Neither sponsors nor catechists can serve effectively if they themselves are not open to the change and transformation that working with new Christians can bring into their own lives. We feel truly blessed as pastoral leaders when a person in one of these leadership roles remarks to us in these (or similar) words: "Tonight, in our small group, I had that passage opened to me in a way I've never seen it before. The questions that the seekers brought were really challenging to me. Thanks for giving me this opportunity to grow in my own life of faith." We hear this more often than one might think.

The calm and accepting atmosphere that a leader who is non-anxious creates is the perfect environment for small group Bible study. In such a welcoming space, conversations flourish and faith is nurtured in the catechumenal model. In many other methods by which newcomers are initiated into Christian life, we as leaders often come only from the perspective of information download. Such theory and practice goes something like this: we have a certain amount of information, ideas, doctrine, and lifestyle to impart; we have a curriculum to follow, a plan to put in place.

But just as the Ethiopian brought new life to Philip, and just as the woman at the well opened the eyes of the disciples, so our eyes can be opened by those who come to study the Scriptures with us for the first time. This was certainly true for us in the case of Kathryn. It has been the case for us with many other newcomers to faith as well. A friend from a Roman Catholic parish who serves as a catechist told me recently of an inquiring woman who witnessed powerfully in her small group—as a candidate! She told her group of her years of visitation ministry in the local jail. Not only did her work in the catechumenate allow her to transform that work in her own mind as the work of Christ, but it also initiated an entirely new ministry within her new congregation.

After her baptism, she enlisted many others in weekly visits to the jail, and through her leadership the ministry has been broadened and strengthened.

In our process in Seattle, pastors identify, recruit, and train the catechists for small group leadership. Then we do our best to get out of the way. Those who attend workshops with us or to whom we offer training are often surprised to learn that neither of us has ever attended a small group. The training we offer our lay catechists is not extensive. Many of them, having now served for a dozen years or more, have developed their own ministry style for their small groups and would likely have much to teach us if the roles were reversed. But in the early days of The WAY, we found it helpful to offer clergy-to-catechist sample discussion starter questions on each Sunday's text as well as other ideas and suggestions for keeping the small groups targeted and vibrant. Care must be taken, however, to always remember as a catechist that the purpose of the small group is to embrace and address the questions that come from the small group's members. As difficult as this paradigm is to accept, we have discovered again and again that the newcomers' questions as well as their insights are the true locus of the Spirit's breath in faith formation.

In an early training video produced by the ELCA for the catechumenate, a lay catechist from a sister congregation in Washington quips, "I don't have a degree in theology; heck, I don't even have a degree in fishing."[1] His point is well taken. The goal of the small group leader is not to impart knowledge but rather to create an open and welcoming place where longtime and newly forming Christians can sit together with the Scriptures resounding in their ears. By listening together, they can discern what God's Word is leading them to embrace as a shared ministry of the Gospel. Men and women mature in faith, possessive of a calm spirit, and compassionate toward others are therefore the best candidates in your parish to fill the role of catechists. Beyond

1. Nelson et al., *Welcome to Christ*. This video teaches the basics of the catechumenal process and is available for download on the ELCA Web site.

that, your local situation and the ethos of your congregation will be much more informative of a model of lay Bible study leadership than any other characteristics that could be discussed here.

In much the same way, those who are chosen as sponsors for candidates for baptism or affirmation should embody these same characteristics of mature faith, a calm and welcoming spirit, and a palpable sense of compassion. As one-to-one guides in the faith, they will be persons with whom the new Christians will share much, and at a highly intimate level. They will become increasingly familiar with one another, develop close bonds of shared faith, pray with one another, and, in many cases, develop a lifelong friendship in Christian community.

We often ask the candidates if they have any preferences in terms of sponsors—would you like contemporaries? Or persons who would be more like faith parents or grandparents to you? As a couple, would you like to be paired with another couple? It has been both surprising and affirming to us just how often the candidates respond with something to the effect of, "Whatever you think is best." It has always been our practice to have sponsors of the same gender, largely because of the physical touch involved in the public rites and because of frequent small group breakouts into conversations involving only the sponsor and inquirer. These pairs become natural outgrowths of the small group work during the period of intense preparation in Lent. All of our sponsors are boundary-trained and chosen because they are knowledgeable about healthy personal boundaries. Again, local circumstance as well as an ever-changing understanding of gender roles across the denominational spectrum will inform how each congregation decides to handle this issue. For each congregation, different criteria will apply as they decide about gender pairings when making sponsor matches.

How are sponsors nurtured and trained? In the early days of our practice, our training was more formal, which was likely the best approach at the time. But as a growing cadre of both sponsors and catechists has developed, we see training as less and less necessary. Our training often consisted more in telling people what they already knew about how to interact with others than it did in any sort of biblical or theological instruction. It took a while for us to convince both potential sponsors and potential catechists that there was no need for them to be biblical scholars, but time has tested the truth of our assertions and allowed us to build a great deal of interest in these ministries.

As time has given us the grace of years of experience, people simply *know* what a sponsor or catechist does. Many have either been one or had one. Those who were well sponsored make great sponsors, of course. They know what worked well for them and are often eager, in a spirit of stewardship and gratitude, to pass the gift that they received on to others. We do make a concerted effort each year to be certain that there are new sponsors in the mix. In the course of the year's ministry, we frequently hear comments such as, "I had no idea this ministry was going on among us. I had no idea it could be so meaningful and fulfilling to be a sponsor. Thank you for inviting me. This is the most rewarding work I have ever done at church."

Among the tasks of the catechumenal team, it is the task of the clergy to lead the ritual life that accompanies this annual journey and to hold the vision of what it means to be a congregation committed to forming faith. Over and over again, we sit with potential candidates and talk with them about the process we are about to invite them to participate in. While we often anticipate the response, "You want us to do *what* for *how long?*" we are often graced by responses such as, "It sounds like this is really important. Thank you for inviting us to take this so seriously."

For too long, we as clergy have not held the Gospel's demand for discipleship in the esteem that it deserves. While we often complain about how willing our congregational members seem to be to make large commitments to sports leagues, work, recreation, or other endeavors, our response has often been to make being a member of a church as easy and as painless as possible. Yet this is not true to the Gospel of Christ, who continually reminded those who would follow him that to do so means to follow in the way of the cross. It has been our experience that by asking much of those who desire to follow Jesus, we all receive much in return. The Gospel promise is true. As pastors and lay leaders holding, espousing, and believing this vision—and working together in our respective roles—we believe that the church's ministry is strengthened and the world more effectively served by lay people and clergy alike.

13

God's Work Alive in the World

VERY EARLY IN MY ministry I attended a pastoral leadership conference at which the late Rev. Dr. William Lazareth was the keynote speaker. His topic, spread across three lectures, was pastoral responsibility, and his refrain—"What do your stoles mean?"—has stuck with me for more than twenty-five years. His point, of course, was that we are ordained for a purpose and that there *are* responsibilities that come with being the theological leader of a community of faith.

One of the greatest gifts of Martin Luther's rediscovery of baptismal theology at the time of the Reformation was helping the Christian community see the depth and breadth of baptism's gifts for all people, not just the clergy. He helped the church discover for a new age that *all* God's people are ordained. The ordination of each person happens at the baptismal font. We are all ordained in baptism into a life of service.

So I have come to broaden and reappropriate Lazareth's lecture theme since my involvement with The WAY. I now see more clearly that laypeople have stoles, too. What do *your* stoles mean?

We have learned over and over again in congregational life that the word *liturgy* means "the work of God's people." But The WAY has helped us learn that our Sunday worship is not the beginning, the middle, and the ending of that work. The real work begins when God's people go into the world to live their daily lives as parents and partners, as lawyers and welders, as decision-makers in the boardroom and in the bedroom. Laypeople's stoles may be tucked beneath their shirts and blouses rather than worn on top of albs, but the baptismal waters certainly ordain the sons and daughters of God into a ministry that is carried out each and every day in vocational living. And the world is watching. Believe me, in a secular city such as Seattle, where many people are not merely indifferent to the church but skeptical or even hostile toward it, the world is watching.

That watching begins with what we do together on Sunday morning. *See how they love one another*, the apostle wrote in the letter to John. It must be obvious with every word and every action of our weekly worship together that we are in love with our God and in love with one another. Love is a serious, thoughtful activity involving commitment, faith, intention, gravity, and joy. As worship planners, the last thing on our minds is to plan a liturgy that is *fun*. The most engaging liturgy imaginable is that which takes the ancient, sacred Word of God and brings it to life to the best of our ability for a time and a people radically different from those to whom it was originally spoken or written. While we may live in a radically different time, we share an inescapable similarity with the ancients—our deep, original sin and our crying need for God's mercy.

If The WAY has taught us nothing else, it has certainly taught us as a faith community that weekly worship stands at the center of all we say and do as God's people. We are first and foremost created for the praise and worship of God, and gathering each Sunday around Word and Sacrament is the greatest joy and the greatest privilege a community of faith could ever have. We gather in the firm conviction that through the words of Scripture and through their dramatic portrayal in our liturgy of worship, God will act once more among us. God will show us the power and presence of God's Word. One of the things that draws us back to worship week after week is the firm conviction that God will surprise us once again.

Worship is the training ground from which men and women of faith are propelled into the world to live in it for the next 167 hours. They are sent to live as they have just lived together for one hour in the most intentional and concentrated way with God and with God's people. At each liturgy God's people are encouraged—by a peer, not a pastor—"Go in peace! Serve the Lord!" And at the joy of the opportunity, having thus been prepared, God's people respond, "Thanks be to God!"

In their seminal work *Lutheranism,* Eric Gritsch and Robert Jenson spend quite a bit of time unpacking the word *of* in the phrase "ministry of the Gospel." Almost everyone seems to understand that disciples of Jesus have a ministry to bring the Gospel to a world in need. But *Lutheranism* challenges us to go deeper, further. We all also have a "ministry *of* the Gospel" in the sense of caring for the Gospel itself. Practicing Christians are called each and every day of our lives to minister *to* the Gospel. That is to say, to the best of our abilities we are called to demonstrate by our lives that the Gospel is *this*, not *that*. It is honesty and not deception. It is mercy and not judgment. It is sacrifice and not personal gain. In living our lives in such a way as these choices imply, we are ministering *to the Gospel itself,* inasmuch as we are witnessing with our lives to the world of the power, the integrity, and the beauty of God's ever-abiding love for us in Jesus Christ.[1]

For every person of God there will come a time of difficult, challenging decision-making. Shall I undergo another round of chemotherapy, or not? Can I trust God to take the risks that are certainly evident if I go over my boss's head and report her misconduct to human resources? Are the things that my fellow tenth graders are asking me to do appropriate? Can I find it deep within myself to forgive him? Do we have the courage as a family to give 10 percent of our income away to others? These and thousands of other daily decisions are on the horizon for any Christian, new or old. Being formed in faith by a community of faith gives us a

1. Gritsch and Jenson, *Lutheranism,* 119.

context out of which to respond, with our best wisdom of the way and the will of God for our lives.

This is what our stoles mean, all of them: The stoles of the pastor and the stoles of the people, the stoles of adults and children, young and old, rich and poor, gay and straight, well educated and differently abled. *All* God's people have a call to live as best we can, each day of our lives, according to the Word and the promises of God.

The WAY is not perfect. It does not magically turn us into a people of faith who do all things right or well. But in a complicated, fast-paced, and increasingly secular world, it *does* offer men and women who are new to faith an intentional period of prayer and study to prepare for their first steps of God's work in a real world. It does much the same for those who were baptized long ago but who left behind their active lives of discipleship. These are men and women like you and me, like Kathryn, Harrison, Robert, Maria, and Jared, Kevin and Anzara and their daughters, who have benefited from what it has had to offer them. But even more amazing is the renewal and new life that has come to each and every member of our community of faith as we have done what we felt called to do. We have done our best to surround Christians in formation with the gifts of honesty and truth, expectation and anticipation. And together we walk hand in hand—waiting, hoping, watching—to see what God will reveal to us next in our journey together along The WAY. And time and time again we are amazed by just how the Spirit's breath blows into us, and gives us life.

14

Afterword

THE FIRST-GRADE LINE LEADER of the entering group looked up at our Children and Family Minister and said, "I don't have any bones." It was his way of saying what everyone else was feeling: "I think I'm going to faint." The quick and apt reply of the teacher was perfect: "Well, just take your skin and your muscles and lean up against this wall, and let's see what happens next." It was a loose translation of Isaiah 40:31, the kind of translation a first grader could understand when ancient biblical words just wouldn't do: "Those who wait upon the LORD shall renew their strength."

This is what happened next. No one fainted on that fateful Lenten Wednesday evening. A broken font for our church, much like a broken bone for an individual, gave us an opportunity to be strengthened. In the end, it wasn't about the fancy blown glass. It wasn't about the beautiful, handcarved, wooden stand. It wasn't even about spilled holy water. It was about children of God, their formation in faith, and the opportunity for us all to live into the love and grace of Jesus that forever surrounds us. We learned again that night that we so often fail to experience grace as fully as we might.

The children navigated around the broken glass and got themselves assembled on the steps of the church, just as they always do on Wednesday evenings for the ten-minute closing worship. A couple of moms mopped up the water, a dad righted the unharmed wooden stand, and someone sent for the custodian. Most important of all, the skilled and faithful choir director pointed the kids ahead to the coming Sunday's story of the prodigal son. There was never a time when unconditional love and forgiveness offered to a child far from home meant so much. They weren't just hearing about it; they were living it.

As the choir director told the story, I was scrambling in the kitchen to find a fancy cut-glass bowl that I knew was in a back cupboard somewhere. I was pretty sure it would fit right into the cavity where the recently shattered bowl had been. When I got back to the sanctuary with the sparkling cut-glass punch bowl hidden under a towel, I asked the kids to close their eyes for just a minute and sing one of their favorites: "I've Just Come from the Fountain." When they opened up their eyes, grace was in full view. It was unmistakable. The baptismal bowl was ready and waiting for worship once again. And to children's eyes, the cut glass shone like diamonds, far outdoing its handblown predecessor. All things had been made new.

With the parable of the prodigal son fresh in their memories, I pointed them toward a favorite verse of mine, 2 Corinthians 5:17: "If anyone is in Christ, there is a new creation; the old has passed away, behold the new has come." It was a mystery beyond the understanding of any child or adult in that room, newcomer or seasoned Christian, that 2 Corinthians 5:17 was the second lesson for the coming Sunday, complementing the prodigal son text in Luke 15.

What we do at Phinney Ridge Lutheran Church is not all that remarkable or innovative, but I believe that it is a faithful response to the Gospel for our day, time, and place. It is what we are called as the Church to do: we keep people from fainting. In the press of everyday life, for those who are new disciples of Christ and those who have been a part of the Church for a lifetime, when life becomes overwhelming or unbearable, we do what God asks of us—we point one another to the Gospel of Jesus. Whether our bones are weak or weary, young or old, robust or brittle, we all need what only Christ can give: the refreshing and renewing breath of the Spirit's grace that has its beginning in the waters of baptism.

The WAY is one congregation's reappropriation of one of the Church's oldest gifts: the gift of walking side by side with one another toward a deeper, richer, fuller relationship with God. It is not perfect, this postmodern project of ours—far from it. But for our congregation, located in one of the most socially liberal, religiously skeptical neighborhoods of one of America's most secular cities, we have found that The WAY works. We minister to thoughtful, inquiring people. They are physicians and engineers, retired fishermen and diesel mechanics. They are truck drivers, cutting-edge cancer researchers, and technical assistants at Amazon.com. People in our congregation were in on the ground floor of Microsoft. Some landscape gardens for a living while others provide in-home childcare. Men and women who come on Sunday mornings with hands outstretched for a bit of grace continue to innovate at Google, or have given their blood, sweat, and tears to get Boeing's 787 Dreamliner in the air. They live out their baptismal vocation by teaching sociology at the University of Washington or English in the local middle school, and they want to know: How do you have a faith these days and come to terms with a flawed creation? Was there really a man named Noah floating in a boat, or a Moses meeting God to convey commandments on stone tablets, or a Jonah caught but undigested in the belly of a whale? And what about Jesus? Truly human *and* truly divine? Born of a virgin? Risen from the dead? Really?

The WAY takes seriously the doubts, fears, and questions of a new generation of disciples. We sit with those questions and admit to one another that we do not have all the answers but would love to be a part of the journey through the questions, together with one another and in the presence of our living God. And The WAY celebrates our common life, as we are richly and deeply immersed in the Word and Sacraments week in and week out.

When the most basic foundations of faith topple to the ground and shatter into a million pieces, there is something left to build upon: the Word and the Sacraments, the community that grace has built, the assurance that we are all in this together and, best of all, that God is in it with us. This is a story of breath blown over dry bones, of sons and daughters welcomed home, of lives shattered and put back together by a community that loves one another. Because we have been so intentional about committing our lives to one another as faith begins or is rekindled, we can trust to be told these stories again and again. And little by little, as surely as the sun rises in the east day after day, the love of God is renewed and re-created among us. It is as tangible in our shared lives as Ezekiel's words themselves, "I will put my Spirit within you, and you shall live."

How We Understand and Practice the Sacrament of Holy Baptism

THE PASTOR'S COLUMN
FROM THE PARISH NEWSLETTER
SUMMER 2011

IN THE LITURGY OF baptism in *Evangelical Lutheran Worship*, we find the following charge to parents and sponsors:

> As you bring your child to receive the gift of baptism, you are entrusted with responsibilities:
>
> > To live with them among God's faithful people,
> > bring them to the word of God and the holy supper,
> > teach them the Lord's Prayer, the Creed,
> >   and the Ten Commandments,
> > place in their hands the holy scriptures,
> > and nurture them in faith and prayer,
> > so that your children may learn to trust God,
> > proclaim Christ through word and deed,
> > care for others and the world God made,
> > and work for justice and peace.
>
> Do you promise to help your child grow in the Christian faith and life?[1]

As a congregation, we have chosen to take great care in the preparation of parents as they anticipate the baptism of their

---

1. *Evangelical Lutheran Worship*, 228.

child. This is true of parents who are new to faith and parents who are new to our congregation. Those seeking to have a child baptized who do not yet have a relationship with our congregation are invited to participate in a season of their own faith formation first as an initial step in being immersed into the community *themselves* and availing *themselves* of the gifts of worship, prayer, formation, and companionship among those to whom their child will belong. This time of formation as Christian parents is an important first step. The truth is, baptism is not a single, one-day event. It is a lifelong commitment on the part of everyone involved, and taking some time to understand and prepare for it is both necessary and prudent.

Baptism is God's gift to parents who, left on their own, could do nothing but struggle in the sacred responsibilities that Christian parenthood demands. The baptism of anyone—child or adult—places that person into the life of a caring community in which the overwhelming tasks of forming a child in faith are shared. Baptism not only makes one a child of God, it makes one a child of the community. *Together* we share in the shaping of that one to live the rest of his or her eternal life in the presence of the almighty, powerful, and loving God and among brothers and sisters in Christ.

With the best that is in us spiritually, theologically, and biblically, Pastor Piro and I believe that this time of preparation is what strengthens our congregation. It forms both parents and children into people who are sturdy enough to withstand the tide of a tempting, secular world. More, a time of preparation for baptism solidifies a parent's relationship to others in the congregation. To these companions in Christ, the parents will turn again and again for advice, for partnership, for prayer, for encouragement in all that lies ahead as a child makes his or her way from the font to their own affirmation as young adults. It is clear to see that much support is gained from parents in our congregation as they are continuously reassured by the presence of others that they are not in this alone.

At the baptismal liturgy, when we read from the bulletin, *We welcome you into the Lord's family, we receive you as a member of the body of Christ,* we are saying much, much more than "Isn't he a cute baby?" or "Doesn't she seem like a nice little girl?" We are saying that from your experience looking into the future of that child toward the terrible twos or life with a thirteen year old, "This is going to take more than just the parents to accomplish." We are in essence committing *ourselves* to the care of this beloved child of God.

Congregations grounded in a rich understanding of what baptism means, how it connects us to one another, and its importance as an act involving all of us, are strong congregations. The strength of the body of Christ is what it takes to bring young Christians, as we say in the liturgy, *to the water of life and to the bread and cup of blessing.*

This is why we both offer and insist on careful, thoughtful, prayerful planning as a baptism approaches. The depth and seriousness of the promises that parents, sponsors, and the congregation make demand such loving thought and care. We are wise and compassionate as a congregation to provide a time for making connections. Together, we walk side by side as partners, charged with the care of a new member of God's family. God asks a lot from us. But then, God also provides the grace by which we can respond and grow into the responsibilities that lie before us.

APPENDIX 2

Ideas, Questions, and Reflections for Getting Started with the Catechumenate in your Parish

THESE IDEAS AND SUGGESTIONS are offered for a large cross-section of readers whose parish experiences will be vastly different. They are not intended as a step-by-step guide for what might happen in each parish considering the catechumenate. These suggestions will best be used by reading through them as a sort of checklist, imagining as pastor or parish leader whether or how they might apply to one's own local situation and then moving through them to imagine and build a strategy appropriate to one's own setting and goals.

CONVERSATION ABOUT SACRAMENTAL LIFE

With pastoral staff, congregation council, worship or evangelism leadership teams, spend some time in intentional conversation and study about the sacramental practices of your parish. Do the practices, rituals, teaching, and time invested match the theological gravity of the sacraments as true means of grace—moments in which God's unconditional promise of presence, love, and support is unmistakably celebrated?

1. Lead a six-week Bible study on each of the sacraments, exploring their biblical roots, the early church's experi-

ence, the modifications in your denomination borne of the Reformation, and your parish's present practice.

2. Include a twenty-minute education and discussion period of the sacraments in the agenda of your worship and evangelism teams and your congregation council for the next twelve months.

3. Engage in congregational prayer that God's grace would be more significantly and tangibly revealed to the assembly through the sacraments.

4. Provide brief educational pieces in the Sunday worship bulletin that help the assembly to make baptismal and eucharistic connections between the various parts of the service. For example, explain the connections between baptism and the rite of confession and forgiveness.

5. Consider present baptismal practice. Are baptisms celebrated within the context of weekly worship? Why or why not? Is it possible to group baptisms into larger parish celebrations on those days in the church year that specifically uplift and support baptismal theology such as All Saints' Sunday, the Baptism of our Lord, the Vigil of Easter, and Pentecost?

6. Discuss and discover ways in which the celebration of baptism in your parish can be more focused on the entire assembly. While this is an important day in the life of one or several individuals, it is an equally important celebration and day of solemn, joyful responsibility for every parish member.

7. Consider the ways in which baptismal and eucharistic education, Bible study, imagery, and play are teaching the children of the parish sound theological principles and healthy patterns around their own sacramental life and that of the entire Christian community.

8. Where is your font and how is it used? Could it be more central? Is it always filled with water? Why or why not? Is water ever poured into the font at occasions such as confession, burial, marriage? In what ways could you imagine making the font and water more prominent in parish life?

9. What patterns are established for parents of newborns to receive information about baptism, its gifts and its responsibilities?

10. What patterns are established for teens and adults who are seeking baptism and who wish to learn more about its practice within your parish's life? Might this be the time to put some policies into place?

11. What are the ways in which baptism and eucharist can be more fully celebrated so as to give witness to their promised presence of Christ among the gathered assembly?

12. In what ways does your Web presence give witness to the centrality of baptism and eucharist in the life of the congregation?

GET THE EASTER VIGIL IN PLACE

It's hard to imagine a catechumenal process in a congregation that does not celebrate the Great Vigil of Easter. Likewise, it's hard to imagine a congregation of any size or description in which the vigil could not be celebrated in some fashion. If there is not a history or tradition of the vigil in your parish, work together as leaders to discover how to get a vigil into place. What would it take to initiate such a practice? How could the inclusion of this timeless Christian liturgy, with its central focus on baptism and its connections to the ancient rituals of pascha (passage), change and encourage a richer understanding of baptism and its gifts among your community in Christ?

1. Consider a year of study with the worship team or parish council on the history, biblical roots, and practice of the Easter vigil.

2. Lead a Bible study series using the twelve appointed texts for the Easter Vigil as the study materials.

3. Incorporate elements of the vigil in regular worship services; for example, baptismal remembrance, creative storytelling of the Scripture texts, or choral or congregational responses to a Bible reading.

4. Begin simply. Schedule the first vigil for early in the evening on the Saturday before Easter. Choose just one of the elements with which to begin—perhaps storytelling of two or three texts and a baptismal remembrance followed by special refreshments and conversation.

5. Visit a vigil in another parish, perhaps even a parish that is not of your own denomination.

6. Make use of video resources of the vigil liturgies of other parishes.

START WITH YOUR CONFIRMATION CLASS

Most congregations are eager to have a vibrant and compelling educational experience for young men and women who are preparing to affirm their baptism and participate in the rite of confirmation. Whether that process takes six weeks or six years in your parish, introducing the congregation to some of the rites, principles, and practices of the catechumenate through the youth participating in confirmation ministry might be a useful strategy for your parish.

1. What is the nature of confirmation education in your parish? In what ways does it reflect the importance of baptism, and how does it point to the affirmation of baptism as the core reason for a young person's participation in this time of intentional education?

2. Is there a mentor process in place for your confirmation ministry? Can you imagine a way in which such a process might lay the groundwork for sponsorship of adult catechumenal candidates in the future?

3. Does your denomination offer rites for the catechumenate that could be easily adapted for use with confirmation students? For example, could a Rite of Welcome and the presentation of a Bible mark the beginning of a confirmation student's journey through their preparations for affirmation of baptism?

4. What pieces are already in place to bridge the time between a young person's baptism and his or her entry into confirmation instruction? Are these seen as separate events, or more of a continuing process of growth in grace?

5. In what ways are young people encouraged to participate in parish leadership as a sign of the ministry of all the baptized? Is there opportunity among your worship leadership teams for elementary and middle school students to serve as lectors, assisting ministers, choir singers, or intercessors?

6. While many parishes decry the lack of children and youth in their parishes, few pray that children and youth will come. What is your parish's practice of prayer around this invitational hospitality?

7. How might you imagine that your entire congregation could become more fully involved and invested in the ministry of confirmation, which often takes place be-

hind closed doors between a small group of youth and the pastor or lay leader?

8. When the rite of confirmation is celebrated, how does the celebration give witness to the joys and responsibilities of baptismal living? How might those aspects be enhanced among your worshiping community liturgically? Here are a few suggestions:

- Include those about to affirm their baptisms in the prayers of the congregation for several weeks leading up to the day of confirmation.

- Have the affirmers presented to the congregation by a familiar, beloved Sunday School teacher or other older adult who has nurtured these young men and women in their faith over the years.

- Have each family/sponsor group bring the affirmer's baptismal candle and pass it from parent or sponsor to affirmer with these or similar words, "In faith, I turn to Christ."

- Have each confirmation student write or artistically/musically prepare a Statement of Faith for his or her confirmation day. Display these statements prominently.

- Have baptismal sponsors, parents, and other parish leaders participate in the laying on of hands for those affirming their baptisms.

- Instruct the congregation (orally, in the bulletin, through prior classes) as to their role in welcoming the newly affirmed into the assembly.

- Use members of the confirmation class as lectors, eucharistic ministers, and other servers on the Sunday of confirmation and immediately thereafter.

9. Compare and contrast what is expected of youth as they affirm their baptism and how that rite is celebrated among adults. If there are differences, why? And what do those differences say about the ways in which both youth and adults are regarded as full members of the body of Christ by virtue of their baptism?

10. Is the curriculum used in preparing young people for the affirmation of baptism lectionary-based? As parish leaders, discuss how a lectionary-based curriculum helps students feel greater connections between their worship life, their class work, and their everyday lives. Does the curriculum that you are using have strong biblical and sacramental foundations? This is essential for connecting worship life to a life of service as a disciple of Jesus Christ.

EVEN WITH JUST ONE INQUIRER

Often the idea of the catechumenate sounds very appealing, but especially in smaller parishes, the objection often arises that there are simply no new people to lead to the waters of baptism and life in Christ. "Our congregation hasn't received a new member, let alone baptized an adult, in recent memory. Why would we want or need such a process?" Even if you have just one person who is inquiring about life as a disciple of Jesus, this process could be ideal for both parish and newcomer. Moreover, it places a structure in motion that makes your congregation more visitor-friendly and inquirer-ready. The practice of the catechumenate positions your congregation as a welcome place for seekers. There is no need to rehearse here the statistics of how quickly the pool of nobelievers is expanding. As congregations, it is incumbent upon us to be ready to welcome those who come in search of Christ. Consider the following:

1. Are there persons in your community who might be more open to exploring a life of discipleship with Christ if they heard that there was a process of study, mentorship, and prayer in place in your congregation to support them in their time of inquiry and preparation for baptism?

2. Are there spouses in your congregation who attend worship or other parish activities occasionally but have never been baptized?

3. Could a single parent or a couple coming to inquire about the baptism of their child be your first catechumenal candidate(s)?

4. Can you imagine people in your parish's service area who are baptized but still seeking adult renewal of their faith? For many, opportunities to both study Scripture and share faith experiences ended in adolescence. There may even be such persons already actively involved in your congregation's life—perhaps even among your parish's leaders.

5. Can you envision two persons in your parish who could sit with one or two persons inquiring into the faith and, with pastoral supervision, offer them Bible study and mentorship in the basics of Christian faith: worship, the Scriptures, prayer, and ministry in daily life?

TAKE YOUR LEADERSHIP TEAM
THROUGH THE PROCESS

Perhaps the section above does not match your parish's circumstances at all. If that is the case, consider instead the implementation of the catechumenal process through a leadership team in your congregation. Over the period of six months or a year, choose a group of willing parish leaders whose lives could be greatly enhanced as they take an intentional sabbatical from administrative parish responsibilities and apply that same time and energy to spiritual enrichment instead.

1. Could your parish council dedicate an hour each month for a twelve-month period to the intentional time of Bible study and shared prayer in the fashion of catechumenal training with the pastor as the catechist? Could their time of study be punctuated and made a part of the assembly's worship and prayer through the use of the rites of the catechumenate adapted for such an experiment?

2. Is there a Bible study group that might be converted into a catechumenal style for a set period of time? Could you imagine using the Rite of Welcome at public worship in which each member receives a Bible (even if it's their own, well-used one!) as a way to mark the beginning of this new journey of faith?

3. Do you have persons in your parish who inquire about ways in which to share their faith more effectively in daily life? Are there people for whom an intentional time of training in witness and testimony might lay some foundational work for catechumenal ministries?

SUPPLEMENT YOUR CONGREGATION'S PRAYER LIFE

I have never been a part of a call process in which these two hopes have not been shared for the congregation's future: we want to bring in more members, and we want to attract more youth. Nor have I been a part of a call interview in which I have not asked, "Have you prayed about this?" After some foot shuffling, one brave soul usually offers, "Well, not really." Few parishes have. It's such an obvious foundational piece that we all often miss it, but it is foundational. God does answer our prayers, and over time prayer also forms the will and the actions of the people. Sooner or later, we begin to think together as a community, how will God bring other people among us if we don't invite them or aren't prepared to receive them?

1. Is the desire to welcome and receive new Christians listed among the prayer concerns of your parish?

2. Do the weekly prayers of the people at worship include petitions for new men, women, and children to become a part of your community of faith?

3. Is the receiving and welcoming of new Christians a part of the regular opening and closing prayers of the evangelism leadership team and the parish council?

ATTEND A CATECHUMENAL TRAINING EVENT

Most congregations will find that the best way to become immersed in and prepared for leadership of catechumenal ministries is by attending a training event. Such events are held in various denominational gatherings, are offered through the NAAC (North American Association of the Catechumenate), and are held at Phinney Ridge Lutheran Church in Seattle. To learn more, visit www.catechumenate.org and www.prlc.org.

APPENDIX 3

Three Faith Formation Sermons from the Lenten Season

+LENT 2, SERIES B

Genesis 17:1–7, 15–16
Psalm 22:23–31
Romans 4:13–25
Mark 8:31–38

IN THE SUMMER OF 1974, I spent twelve weeks abroad as a foreign exchange student in Kabul, Afghanistan. It was the first time I'd ever flown in an airplane, the first time I'd been much outside of York County, Pennsylvania, and the first time I'd ever been with a group of other high school students who actually felt like peers.

After ten days of intense orientation in both New York City and Istanbul, the seventeen of us landed at the Kabul airport, were met by our host families and quickly whisked into private cars, taxis, or bicycles for our separate journeys to what was about to become "home."

The next hour was unbelievable. Our driver poured recklessly through the city's streets, which teemed with walkers, camels, shepherds and their flocks, some other cars, and bicyclists.

The air was accented by honking horns, bleating and baaing animals, and blaring music both live and recorded. There were more times than I care to remember that we came this close to another car, a pedestrian, a biker, some sheep. It was a ride I will never forget.

By the time we reached our family compound and servants came to open the gate at the honking of our car horn, I had seen fresh meat hanging in the open air market, women roaming the streets completely covered in chaderies, brilliantly painted trucks, mosques, breathtaking surrounding mountains.

This was not what I was expecting. I was trying hard just to breathe. It was clear I wasn't in southern Pennsylvania anymore, and that I was eighteen and incredibly alone. I had no idea when I would see one of my new American friends again. I wanted my mom. Though I didn't know it at the time, I was in shock. Culture shock. And I stayed there for several days, maybe even weeks. To cross from one culture to another in such a short period was too much.

I was not and am not alone in this cross-cultural experience. I would find out later that some of my fellow exchange students had traveled the same journey through the capital city as I had, only on bicycles or in rickshaws. When they got "home," there was no porcelain toilet like the one just off my bedroom, but a shared hole near the back of the small property that their host family called home.

I am not telling you this story to evoke pity or awe these thirty-odd years later. I'm telling you this story because cross culture shock is common to the human experience. It happens whenever one person is taken from his or her own native way of thinking and experiencing life, and is transported into something entirely new.

I am telling you this story because it is exactly what is happening to Peter and the disciples in the Gospel text for today. They are being transported into something entirely new. They are being taught by Jesus that their new culture is a culture of the cross. And this is not what they were expecting.

"If any want to become my followers, let them deny themselves, take up their cross and follow me."

This, on the heels of Jesus' first inkling to the disciples of his own fate: "He began to teach them that the Son of Man must undergo great suffering, and be rejected by the elders, the chief priests, and the scribes, and be killed . . ."

In the space of a few unwelcome words, the tiny band of followers had crossed into a new culture, a new place, the beginnings of a new understanding, but just the beginnings. They could not take it in. Peter argues, others ignore, and some, no doubt, stand wide-eyed in amazement and shock. Culture shock. The shock of cross culture.

It would take three repetitions of Jesus' passion prediction to begin to have the news "take" with the disciples. Today's words from the eighth chapter are repeated again in the ninth, then once more in the tenth. From there the events themselves point to the cross, and still, for the most part, the disciples don't understand. In the end, when they have all scattered and Jesus is alone on Calvary, it is the most unlikely of disciples who is the first to get it. A Roman centurion looks upon the suffering one and proclaims the Gospel for the first time from human lips, "Truly, this man was the Son of God."

God is inviting us to move into a new culture. A cross culture. The culture of the Christ. But it is important to realize that this move will not happen in the twinkling of an eye. Read your text carefully. Jesus *began* to teach them—he *began*. We will not understand, or fully appreciate, or ever really "get" this cross-bearing stuff completely. There will always be vestiges of our native human culture of original sin that cling to us. No matter what Jesus teaches, we will have a voice inside that says, "For me, it's different. I can do this myself. I'm carrying as much cross as I can. Yes, but Jesus, surely you didn't mean suffering . . . did you?"

Abraham and Sarah's connection from Genesis to the Gospel text about cross bearing might seem remote, but it is intimately connected to the idea of transformation and journey. Over the course of their lifetimes—not in a single moment in time—over the course of their lifetimes they were led by God to a new place. A place of faithful obedience. A place of following. A cross-cultural experience so powerful that they took up different names, more fitting to their new lives. A cross-cultural experience so transforming that it made from their old, worn, limp bodies the fertile, life-giving loins from which would flow a multitude of nations.

"If any want to become my followers, let them deny themselves, take up their cross and follow me."

We are invited into the culture of the cross. And it will be a shocking, cross-cultural journey. A learning of a new way of living that will take a lifetime. We will not be model cross bearers by later this afternoon.

Jesus began to teach them. Jesus *began*. Learning to follow takes time. There are a million deaths to die along the way. Deaths to the old way of doing things. Deaths to things that we once thought so important. Deaths to our own wills and ways for the sake of those Christ calls us to serve.

Take up your cross and follow.

Take it day by day. Little by little. Remember, Jesus is only just beginning to teach us.

And little by little the culture of the cross will become more familiar. Less shocking. Over time, even something to embrace.

This is the promise of Christ, who gives us through his cross the countercultural gifts of light out of darkness, speech out of silence, pardon out of injury, healing out of disease, even life out of death.

In the name of the Father, and of the Son, and of the Holy Spirit. Amen.

+LENT IV, SERIES B

Numbers 21:4–9
Psalm 107:1–3, 17–22
Ephesians 2:1–10
John 3:14–21

"MAKE A POISONOUS SERPENT, and set it on a pole; and everyone who is bitten shall look at it and live."

Oh, if only it were so simple! If I could simply erect for you a serpent of bronze, set it on a pole, hold it up, and let your sins be forgiven. I would do it in a heartbeat, if it were possible. Wouldn't that be nice?

Just like us, the people of Moses were caught in a wilderness. It may not have been a wilderness of failed mortgages, climbing unemployment rates, raging, festering Middle Eastern wars against unfamiliar, unseen enemies. But we really have nothing in our lifetimes that they didn't have. The impacts are the same. Mothers and fathers worry about the futures of their children. Old folks wonder if things can get much worse. People wax nostalgically about the good old days and turn to lies and deceit as a way of coping. In short, sin and self-centeredness abound.

And sooner or later the truth comes out—at least it did then. "We have sinned against the LORD. Bail us out, Moses."

"Make a poisonous serpent, and set it on a pole; and everyone who is bitten by their own sin and self-centeredness shall look at it and live."

I have no pole to lift, no serpent of bronze for you to gaze upon. Oh, if only it were so simple.

But the business of sin and forgiveness is not simple. Ages and ages of the human family have learned and relearned the truth of just how difficult and sorrowful our mean, self-centered, and thoughtless actions toward one another can be. But what we have not learned, and what we at some very deep level of our humanity seem unable to learn is how to use the tools and the power that Jesus has given us to live together, to love one another, and to share with the world the sort of unconditional mercy that Christ has come to share with us. With us, and through us to all people.

Sin is serious business. Apparently somewhere along the line, God's people discovered that looking at a bronze serpent on a pole just wasn't doing it for them. Maybe that was because, as St. Paul puts it, the more they sinned, the more they assumed grace would abound, so why bother?

Perhaps life got better and they just forgot their need to do even the simplest of the acts of repentance—looking back toward God and the things that God provides. But likely the most typical reason that we have fallen back in upon ourselves and put away not only the serpents on the poles but every other method of redemption is that we are convinced—*convinced*—that we can be totally self-reliant. Who needs God, anyway?

After the serpent on the pole, which they themselves had demanded, the people demanded to be ruled by judges—a human conception for a very human way of life. So God sent judges. Then the people demanded a king. Again, a very human conception for a very human way of life. So God sent kings. But the kings led in ancient times to the same kinds of social and political crises that we know in our own world. Under kings, nations vie for power and wealth, domination and prestige. There is always someone somewhere trying to undo those who would rule with justice, with an eye toward equality and mercy for all. The prophets warned against such human tendencies, but their words went unnoticed, unheard.

By the time God sent Jesus, the world was too deeply mired in its own sinking sands of sin, and those who remained faithful were among the marginalized and the powerless. This was a situation, like ours, that no serpent on a bronze pole was going to ameliorate. And this is the judgment that the light has come into the world and the people loved darkness rather than light because their deeds were evil.

The crisis of human sin was so great that it took Jesus all the way to the cross. It cost him his life. To make things right again for us, to refashion life in the way that God had first created life to be for us, Jesus stopped at nothing. That's how great the mercy of Jesus is toward us. That's how great.

If ever there was a part of Jesus' way of seeing and being in the world, it is this very thing. To offer up oneself in reconciliation. To give oneself to make things better for others. To die to ourselves that others may have *just a little bit of life*. This is the call and the cost of discipleship in our own day and time.

And that kind of ministry will cost us, too. It is not as simple as hanging a serpent on a pole, waving it around like a magic wand and making things better. To offer ourselves as Jesus offered himself will mean that something in us needs to die. Something we've long held on to—a grudge, an unpaid debt, a conviction that we are right, or an old prejudice, perhaps one that is so deep and so entrenched that we can't even recognize it as a fault of our own.

To be in the world as Jesus was in the world, something in us will have to die.

So who is the sister with whom you need to rebuild a relationship? Who is the coworker who you need to approach with an open mind? Where are the places that the love with which God so loved the world can run through your veins, your words, your courage to make all things new?

No question about it—this will cost you. Something will have to die. It will not be easy to reconcile in and with the world in which we live. Breathing the air of mercy for others as Christ first breathed it for us is the important, necessary, counter-cultural work of the Gospel.

But it is just that—it is the Gospel. And it will set us free.

Because with Jesus there is never a death that is not also accompanied by a resurrection. There is never a dying without a rising. There is never a cross without an empty tomb.

So think of it. Just think of it. We *get* to be the voice of Jesus in the world. We get to be the agents of mercy. We get to be the ones who reach out to others and, with our own words, our own actions, and our own courageous way of being, make all things new.

Oh, that it were as easy as lifting a serpent on a pole! The work of reconciliation in the world is not nor has it ever been so easy.

God so loved the world that he gave his only Son to do this work. And now, God so loved the world that he gave us. Yes, us. Breathe in. Breathe out. The mercy of the crucified and risen Christ is all around us. And now God is asking us to die to ourselves and be alive for others. To breathe the mercy of Christ into a world gasping for fresh air.

In the name of the Father and of the Son, and of the Holy Spirit. Amen.

+MAUNDY THURSDAY, SERIES C

Exodus 12:1–4 [5–10], 11–14
Psalm 116:1–2, 12–19
1 Corinthians 11:23–26
John 13:1–17, 31b–35

NATHAN BENJAMIN WAS ABOUT three when he attended his first Maundy Thursday service. The church was small, so even though I was stripping the altar, I could catch a glimpse of him now and then. He sat in his mother's lap as if transfixed. He couldn't take his eyes off of what was happening. "This is my commandment, that you love one another as I have loved you."

They couldn't take their eyes off of what was happening, either. Nor could they unfasten their hearts, or wrap their minds around Jesus' taking up the towel and basin to kneel at their feet and wash them. This was not the work of a leader, but of a servant. The disciples had only ever known the lowliest in their world to do such a task.

It somehow fit with the strangeness of this man they had come to follow. So many things were spinning out of control by now that anything was possible. Even this. Jesus was kneeling at their feet, and with tender affection and an unmistakable sense of service, he was washing them. "This is my commandment, that you love one another as I have loved you."

The first time I presided at the Eucharist on Maundy Thursday evening here at Phinney, I was disturbed by strange sounds. It took me a while to figure it out, but by the end of the service it dawned on me that the banging and the shuffling, the slamming car doors and the muffled conversation were coming from downstairs at the Food Bank. The Food Bank is open on Thursday evenings, even Maundy Thursday evening, and men and women who don't have enough to eat come and receive from men and women who do have enough the gift of simple, nourishing food for the coming week. "This is my commandment, that you love one another as I have loved you."

Even as the presider on that first Maundy Thursday among you, my mind was making mental notes. This has got to be fixed. We can't have people banging around downstairs and handing out food while such a sacred service is taking place in the sanctuary. The Food Bank needs to have different hours during Holy Week. Check.

On Good Friday almost twenty years ago, at about one o'clock in the afternoon, Nathan Benjamin's mom put him down for his nap, just like she always did at that time of day. Around 2:30, she heard him shuffling around in his room and talking to himself and decided it was time to resume their afternoon routine together. I could never have imagined what she told me she had found.

When Mrs. Benjamin opened Nathan's door, she gasped. Every single thing in his bedroom was gone. There were no books on his shelves, no sheets on his bed, no toys on the floor. He had cleared off the top of his little dresser. Even his favorite blanket was gone. Nathan, what are you doing?

She was stunned by his response. I'm playing church. It took her a few moments to figure it out, but then it dawned on her. Nathan had stripped his bedroom, just as he had seen the church being stripped the night before. This simple, profound action made an impression. It stuck. He was formed in his young and innocent faith by what he had seen. "This is my commandment, that you love one another as I have loved you."

After that first Holy Week here among you in Seattle, I soon forgot about the "disturbance" of the Food Bank clatter on Maundy Thursday. One day of the Easter season stretched into another, then it was summer, next we were celebrating Advent and Christmas, and before I knew it I was standing over the Eucharist again on Maundy Thursday. And there they were, those same unusual sounds. But by this time, I was a little wiser. I had heard many stories about serving in the Food Bank from all of you. I had seen the faces of the men and women who come here for these gifts. I had heard their sincere thank-yous at the Thanksgiving and Christmas distribution days. I was moved to a different place. What I saw and heard and learned and knew among you formed me in my faith. What was going on in the Food Bank on Maundy Thursday was also worship. Worship of a different kind. I remembered that Jesus had once said, "These people honor me with their lips, but their hearts are far from me." It was not so among you. Through the Food Bank workers, you all were carrying out the Maundy, the Mandate, of this Holy Thursday. "Love one another as I have loved you."

Jesus knelt at the feet of his disciples and washed them. He did the work of a servant. By this simple yet deeply profound gesture, he was forming them in faith. Showing them the life that they were to lead once he was no longer with them. It was a gift. His parting gift to them. His final will and testament to who God is, and what God desires us to be. "Love one another."

When I saw Nathan Benjamin's parents in Texas this past November, they told me that he is a sophomore at Texas A&M now. He comes home every couple of weekends with a big basket of laundry and always worships with his parents when he's in town. They're not so sure about those weekends that he spends on campus. But they've never forgotten that Holy Week in 1988, and neither has he. God's way of forming us in faith sticks, and helps us grow into the men and women of righteousness that he longs for us to be. Little by little. Step by step. Day by day.

It is not likely that you will wash anyone's feet today, tomorrow, or any day in the immediate future. Nor that you will give or receive the bread and cup of blessing that is offered by our Lord himself for you, for all, for the forgiveness of sin and the renewal of life. Not likely that you will do or see either of these things any place but here.

But through them, God sends us all into the world. Amid the clutter of slamming doors, the banging and shuffling of broken, chaotic lives, and the muffled conversations, we are called to bring the meaning and connection of Christ, one to another.

Out there in the world, God is sending us to serve, just as Christ has served. By these things we are formed in faith. We are changed. And by them, we live out the Maundy given to all disciples as a final gift. That Maundy, that mandate to love one another as Christ has loved us.

In the name of the Father, and of the Son and of the Holy Spirit. Amen.

Bibliography

Bass, Diana Butler. *Christianity for the Rest of Us: How the Neighborhood Church Is Transforming the Faith.* San Francisco: HarperSanFrancisco, 2006.

Evangelical Lutheran Worship. Minneapolis: Fortress, 2006.

Gritsch, Eric W., and Robert W. Jenson. *Lutheranism.* Philadelphia: Fortress, 1976.

Huck, Gabe, and Mary Ann Simcoe, editors. *A Triduum Sourcebook.* Chicago: Liturgy Training Publications, 1983.

Jenson, Robert. *Visible Words: The Interpretation and Practice of Christian Sacraments.* Philadelphia: Fortress, 1978.

Lutheran Book of Worship. Minneapolis: Augsburg, 1978.

Nelson, Paul et al., editors. *Welcome to Christ: Lutheran Rites for the Catechumenate.* Minneapolis: Augsburg Fortress, 1997.

Turner, Paul. *The Hallelujah Highway: A History of the Catechumenate.* Chicago: Liturgy Training Publications, 2000.

Weems, Ann. *Kneeling in Jerusalem.* Louisville: Westminster John Knox, 1992.